# LIFE
# DEATH
# LIFE

**FLOYD FAUST**

The Upper Room

The Upper Room      Nashville, Tennessee

# LIFE/DEATH/LIFE

Scripture quotations, unless otherwise noted, are from the Revised Standard Version of the Bible, copyrighted 1946, 1952, and © 1971 by the Division of Christian Education, National Council of the Churches of Christ in the United States of America, and are used by permission.

UR-356-10-0177

# Table of Contents

# Introduction

This book is born out of deep sympathy with the vast number of men, women, children, and young people, whose health, happiness, and usefulness are impaired or destroyed by their inability to accept death and dying. It is not an academic effort beamed at those Paul described as interested only in "telling or hearing some new thing." Its aim rather is to help open hearts and minds to God's ways of answering our prayers, particularly when our "thorn in the flesh" is not miraculously removed, the circumstance of illness or death is not circumvented, the realities of our situation will not adjust to us and we with God's help are compelled to adjust to them.

It is my purpose here to set forth clearly the Christian belief in life after death, grounded firmly in sound scholarship and presented graphically in experiences gleaned from real-life situations. Having been trained in philosophy and religion, I have researched extensively the subjects of death and dying and of life after death under academic supervision. Across several decades I have served as a parish minister in a large city church and my wife as a clinically trained hospital chaplain, work which kept us both immersed in sorrows, acquainted with grief, and with the need for a supportive faith to see these circumstances through. Then, having lost our fourteen-year-old daughter in a tragic and ill-fated tonsillectomy, I am able to affirm to the suffering and sorrowing, "I have sat where you sit!"

It is out of the crucible of triumph in tragedy and a profound appreciation for the help received from the Christian belief in life after death, that I attempt here to share this faith. It is offered in the hope that others now walking through the valley of the shadow may find it helpful in opening their lives to God's help, that they, too, may be led through the desert and wilderness of doubt and despair into God's promised land of faith, hope, love, and readjustment to reality.

FLOYD FAUST

# Chapter
# 1

## My Belief in
## Life After Death

A generation ago a New England preacher told a class of seminary students, "If you want to deliver a sermon of universal appeal, preach to broken hearts."

Is it possible that you are young, or perhaps middle-aged, enjoying good health and absorbed in the joys and anticipations of vigorous living? When you read the title of this book, did you exclaim, "Look at me! Do I strike you as the type that would be interested in the subject of death or dying?" To this I would answer, "Don't go away!"

I am a boating enthusiast. Each of us must have somewhere a peaceful retreat from the tensions of involvement with life in the city, and mine is a cottage and boat on the shores of Lake Erie. Sometimes in midsummer the surface of that water is as smooth as plate glass—calm, serene, and inviting. What a joy to turn the bow of the boat into that placid surface, open the throttle, and feel the stern of the craft sink and the bow rise! Then with more power, the bow drops down, the stern rises, and the entire craft planes, skimming exhilaratingly across the surface, seeming hardly to touch the water. What a refreshing delight! But on another occasion that same lake may be wild and windblown, and I will find myself sitting behind the wheel among waves higher than my head. I thoroughly enjoy this experience also.

I have discovered, however, that a great many persons fail to derive from this latter ride the joy it affords me. Why not? Last summer while in the midst of one of those roll and spray cruises, the answer came through to me strong and clear. The difference is, *I can swim,* and indeed I delight in doing so. Some might call, "Look out! Don't you know that boat may sink!" But I would answer, "I have life preservers aboard and I can swim. I don't want to see this boat go down, and I have no feeling I'm endangering it in this particular chop. I insist on such security measures so that the fear of capsize will not sabotage my enjoyment of the ride." Do you understand now why I insist that knowing how to swim is a prerequisite to enjoyment of a boat ride? Furthermore, the more treacherous the sea the more necessary is swimming proficiency if we are to have a happy cruise. In the same way, I am convinced that no one really can enjoy a single day of living until he has settled satisfactorily with the inevitability of dying. Would you tap me on the shoulder while I am enjoying myself in some favorable hour of activity and say, "Don't you know that at any moment that body of yours may fall into disrepair, be destroyed by disease or accident, or crumble with age?" My enthusiastic response is, "Let it go when it must. *I can swim!*"

One evening after a lecture, Ralph Waldo Emerson found himself confronted by a wide-eyed lady who hurried down the aisle, seized him by the arm, and exclaimed, "Dr. Emerson! Don't you know the world is coming to an end this year on the 14th of October?" The great Mr. Emerson smiled calmly and said, "O, well, let it go. We can get along without it."

At this point, lest some might gain the impression that I am "otherworldly," let me hasten to deny the accusation. Although I can affirm confidently with Paul, "For me to die is gain," I definitely am in no hurry to take off! This is a wonderful world. There is much yet to be done in helping our Father finish his creation. This is the best world I have ever lived in, and I am enjoying the experience so much I would regret seeing the curtain rung down on a drama so intensely interesting.

A few years ago I was called into a suburb of our city to see one of the fine older ladies of our church. She had suffered a heart attack, and I was advised I might not see her alive again unless I came quickly. I approached her bedside quietly and probably a bit gravely, for I had loved this Christian friend dearly for a quarter of a century. She seemed to be in a coma, so I laid my hand gently on hers. Imagine my surprise when she opened her eyes, looked up at me sharply, and in her usual, quick Welsh dialect said, "Now look young man! Don't you come in here talking to me like an old holy-toned, tear-stained-voiced preacher did to my mother one time!" I was really startled by that, for it was quite a speech to come from one I thought was nearly dead. When I recovered, I asked, "What did the old preacher say to your mother?" Her answer came in the same staccato tones. "Well, my mother had a severe sick spell, and our old minister came to see her. He bent over, took her hand in his, and said in his best funeral tone, 'Aunt Sally, you're ready to go!' My mother rose sharply and said, 'Indeed I'm not ready to go. I like it here!'" To this I respond with a hearty, "Amen!" When God the Creator completed this natural world in which we live, he looked at it and said, "It is good!" I heartily concur with him in that judgment, and I, too, "like it here."

I thank God, however, that as much as I love this present world, my life and happiness are not dependent upon it. A friend expressed this for me quite vividly a few years ago. He told me of an experience he had at his dining room window one afternoon during a violent summer thunderstorm. A few feet away stood a weeping willow tree. He was intrigued as he watched it being tossed and rolled by the strong wind. Suddenly he leaped to his feet. A bird was sitting on one of those tossing limbs, singing at the top of his voice. His first impulse was to say, "You fool bird! Why should you be singing at a time like this? Don't you know that limb may break off and go crashing down at any instant!" Then he reported that the truth of the situation suddenly dawned like a burst of light on his mind, and the secret of that bird's security became clear. He related it in these words, "On the bough that swings there's a bird that sings, because he knows he's got wings!" This states the case with crystal clarity! The bird clings to the branch and appreciates it, but he is able to enjoy it during a threatening storm because "he knows he's got wings" and doesn't have to have it. This is why my belief in life after death contributes to the joy and enthusiasm I bring to and derive from everyday living in these threatening times. Like my ability to swim while boating, or like the wings of the bird on that plummeting bough, my faith constitutes the secret ingredient that gives me spiritual security essential to my enjoyment of life.

Now for the crucial question! What about you? Do you share this faith, this composite of conviction and feeling, to such a degree that it can work this same miracle of peace and security in your life?

Probably no one has given us a clearer picture of what death means to a mature Christian than grand old John Quincy Adams. When that remarkable American was turning four-score years, he was hobbling down the street one day in his favorite city of Boston, leaning heavily on a cane. Suddenly a friend slapped him on the shoulder and said, "Well, how's John Quincy Adams this morning?" The old man turned slowly, smiled, and said, "Fine, sir, fine! But this old tenement that John Quincy lives in is not so good. The underpinning is about to fall away. The thatch is all gone off the roof, and the windows are so dim John Quincy can hardly see out anymore. As a matter of fact, it wouldn't surprise me if before the winter's over he had to move out. But as for John Quincy Adams, he never was better . . . never was better!" With

7

this he started hobbling on down the street, believing without a shadow of doubt that the real John Quincy Adams was not a body that you could ever enclose in a casket or inter in a grave. The real John Quincy was a soul, a spirit, a personality, and for him death was only "moving day," when that spirit of his would move out of an old and no longer properly habitable body. While that earthly tenement in which he had lived for so long certainly would return to the dust from which it came, he himself just as certainly would not do so, for "dust thou art, to dust returnest, was not spoken of the soul!"[1]

What a faith! And how sincerely I hope and pray that you share it. Having for nearly half a century been a Christian minister in a downtown church in a large metropolis, I have come to be pastor to the many individuals and families of the city who have no church home and no pastor of their own. When death suddenly strikes in their lives they will call feverishly for a Christian minister to preside over the last rites for their deceased. In my professional experience I rarely feel so sorry for anyone as for these who oftentimes have built their life's enjoyment and their soul's security on sandbars of human companionship that now is washed away. Suddenly the rains fall, and the earthly companionship that provided the only meaning life held for them is swept away. They have nothing to cling to, no tested and appreciated footing remaining on which they can stand. I have trembled while watching grown men having literally to be torn away from a casket. I have heard them sobbing, "It's terrible to think of you being enclosed there," or at the graveside, "It's horrible to think of leaving you out here." And wouldn't it be? If we really loved someone dearly, the very thought of such a dark, cold, and lonely confinement would be more than the heart could bear. But, thank God, we who are Christian know with a sustaining faith, "My loved one is not in that casket, has never been in it, and is not going to any cemetery." In fact, to a believing Christian a cemetery is the emptiest place in the world. There's just nobody there!

I feel perhaps even sharper pangs of sympathy and sorrow for the family that does have a church home and minister, who turn to him when death comes for assurance and hope and eagerly ask for bread, but receive only a stone. Too often the minister has not thought and prayed this matter through at all, and in consequence has no clear faith adequate for his own life, to say nothing of theirs. Accordingly he only feebly and evasively treats the tragic circumstance with an aesthetic poem or a sentimental song. I am sure that no Christian minister acceptably discharges the responsibility laid on him by his Lord at such an hour unless he so believes, loves, and speaks at a funeral service in such a way that he sends the casket out empty, and the grieving family to their homes looking upward and forward, comforted and expectant.

What a strength this faith provides for those who have chosen to accept it and have cultivated it to full flower in their lives, before there descends upon them the fateful hour when they desperately need it. Some years ago a grand old man came into my study, visibly ill. He was one of the sweet-spirited elders of our congregation who had sat faithfully for years under our Christian teaching. He also had shared deeply in the work and fellowship as well as the worship of his church. Noticing with alarm his apparent illness, I said, "Have you seen a doctor lately?" He shook his head. I suggested, "I have a good friend who is one of the most competent physicians in this city. If I call him will you go see him?" He agreed, and I made the appointment. A short time later the doctor called me to say, "Your old friend was just here, and he isn't going to live but a few days. I'm sure there's nothing anyone can do for him. I didn't tell him this, and I'm sending him back to you. You tell him if you think he should know."

There is much debate in medical and pastoral circles about the wisdom of telling the fact of their condition to patients who are facing what seems to be a terminal illness. In my own experience I make the judgment separately in each individual case, depending heavily upon the emotional and spiritual maturity of the individual and family involved. Repeatedly I have observed fine men and women being denied warm and supporting fellowship with their loved ones at such a time, a relationship which, if it had been honest and intimate, could have meant much to both the dying person and the family. They missed this experience because each felt obligated to play a game with the other and pretend not to know the gravity of the situation, when in fact both would much rather have shared their feelings with each other than to have talked about anything else in the world. It is equally true, however, that some persons would lose their poise completely, blow an emotional fuse, and precipitate a difficult situation for everyone involved if they were advised of their true condition. This occurs when those involved lack the strength of character and the spiritual preparation necessary to face such a crisis calmly. I am sure, therefore, that each decision regarding how much to tell a patient in a time of terminal illness must be made on its own individual merit. One advantage of a long pastorate is the opportunity it provides a minister to know his people intimately enough to make such a judgment with some degree of accuracy. On this basis I was certain this dear old friend should know precisely what the doctor believed was his true condition. Accordingly, I prepared myself spiritually as best I could, and when my friend returned I attempted to prepare him also. Then I told him just what the medical examination had revealed. He sat quietly for a moment, his eyes filling with tears as the revelation registered in his mind. Then he looked up at me, smiled warmly, and said, ''Well now, that's all right! This announcement would have floored me completely if I had heard it a few years ago, but not now. Not since last summer.'' ''Last summer?'' I asked. ''What happened last summer to change your attitude toward a matter as serious as this?''

Then he described how he had been living alone. ''My wife has been gone for fifteen years now, and although I have two fine children, they have their own families and live in distant cities. I haven't wanted them to be bothered with me or my problems. So I admit I've been terribly lonely. Last summer I decided I was homesick. I was born and raised in Vermont and hadn't been back to my old hometown for forty-five years, so I arranged for a vacation. One afternoon in August, tingling with anticipation, I turned my old car down the familiar long hill in New England to the scene of my childhood days. I could hardly wait. I planned to go first to the old country store and hunt up Jim, Bill, and Pete. We used to spend hours swapping stories around the potbellied stove there. Then I would visit the old church where Mother and I were married.''

Then his head dropped. A sad expression came over his face, and he said, ''How can I describe to you the pain of my disappointment when I drove into that little town? I didn't even know the place! The store was gone and a filling station stood on that corner. The church was gone too, and a business block was built up on the site. Finally I parked my car and began walking up and down the street. I couldn't find a soul I knew. I stopped several strangers and asked, 'Don't you remember Jim or Pete or Bill?' They were nice to me. They would ponder and maybe mumble, 'Let me see,' but they couldn't even remember my friends. I was never as homesick in all my life as I was in my old hometown. Finally, with a lump choking me in my throat, I got back in my car and drove out on the hill to the old cemetery. There they were! A big stone by the drive said, 'Jim.' Not far away I found 'Bill' and finally 'Pete' back by the fence. And there was 'Old Uncle Bob!' What a great friend he was to all of us boys at a time in our lives when we needed someone wise in the ways of the world who'd take time to talk to us! I sat on his stone and visited with him awhile. Then I sat down on another stone and just plain cried. I said to myself, 'Brother! The trouble with you is, your world has moved on over to the other side.' All you've told me today is that it's time now for me to move over and join it, and that's all right . . . it's all right.'' He was smiling by now with a light of real joy in his face. Then he added, ''Well, I've got a few things I'll need to do to get ready, and there's one favor I'd like to ask of you. Just keep talking to me so I don't lose this point of view, and I'll walk straight into the sunset with my head up!''

This is the faith of which I have been speaking, set forth in the kind of practical, life-changing attitude that is necessary for all of us if we are to escape heartbreak and dissolution of will in the face of death. This is true whether the death be our own or of someone who means very much to us. It was a great day in her life when Margaret Fuller burst forth with the exclamation, ''I accept the universe!'' Have you come to an agreeable acceptance of death? Although it does not always come according to God's will, when it does it is an angel of mercy that clips the cord and sets us free from an old and no longer properly habitable body that often has become more of a prison than a palace.

# Chapter 2

# Is This the Will of God?

But death does not always come when our life is mature "like a sheaf of wheat in its season." When "this old tenement" is worn out, the Grim Reaper is no longer grim, but quite properly may be welcomed as an angel of liberation and release. Quite often, however, because of an accident or illness, death's sickle strikes down youth; and the older are compelled to say good-bye to the younger. Then life's plan seems cruelly out of joint. Sensitive hearts and minds cry out for answers and often seethe in rebellion when promising children, youths whose life purposes are totally unfulfilled, or young parents desperately needed by their dependent children are cut down. What do Christians have to say under these circumstances?

One morning quite early my study phone rang. A prominent physician in our city was on the line with a request. "Mrs. Lowry underwent surgery two weeks ago," he told me, "and is supposed to be recuperating here in our hospital. But she is not getting well. In fact, she is growing steadily worse and will die if the present trend is not reversed. We have done all we can do for her medically. I believe her problem lies in your field, and I would like you to call on her. I might warn you, however, not to be surprised if she is quite hostile or completely rejects you."

Before noon that day I walked into her room. When I spoke her name I received no reply, not even the slightest recognition of my presence. Quietly I explained to her who I was, that I had heard of her illness and delay in recovering, and had come to visit with her. When I had all but given up and was at the point of leaving, she suddenly came up sharply on one elbow and said, "Why did God take my boy?"

I sensed the passion in her question and attitude and felt certain I was being admitted directly into both the treasure-room and morgue of her life, now in serious disorder from violent invasion. I also felt that this turbulent area I was approaching probably

13

constituted precisely the barrier to her physical recovery the doctors had been seeking.

"Tell me about your boy," I said quietly.

After a time Mrs. Lowry, in words so bitter she fairly spat them at me through clenched teeth, began relating the following story. She had been left with four small children when her husband, a farmer on a small acreage near our city, was drafted into military service and shot down in a fighter plane he was piloting during World War II. She had reassembled her shattered life after that crisis, and by hard work and good management had held the farm and family together nobly for ten years. Her indispensable assistant and mainstay was her oldest son, who had reached his senior year in high school. He not only carried major responsibility for the farm work but was also his mother's strength and support emotionally because of his fine character and mature judgment. Then one windy morning in late spring as he drove the manure spreader around the corner of their barn, the silo blew over on him. He was instantly crushed to death.

By the time Mrs. Lowry reached this climax in her narrative she was so choked with tears and grief she was unable to continue. For several minutes we sat in silence together. Finally she added, "I managed once, ten years ago, to pull my life together and make a new start, but I just cannot and will not do it again. What kind of God is it that would take Ronnie from me just now, when he was so good and was needed so much?"

First of all, I assured her that I understood how she could entertain these feelings, and made clear my acceptance of her and my rapport with her—rebellion, bitterness, and all.

Then I said, "But let me assure you, God did not take your boy."

This brought her straight up in bed. "I expected you to tell me something like that," she responded sharply, "but I'm not a bit impressed. This is the way I've got it figured. If God isn't running this universe, who is? If nobody's running it, I know I don't want to live in it. But if God is in control around here and he didn't take Ronnie, he certainly let it happen and is just as responsible as if he'd planned it and carried it out with his own hand."

Now she became significantly silent. The quietness of an unfathomable loneliness settled on her face, and that faraway look came again into her eyes.

"It is bad enough to lose Ronnie," she finally began saying more to herself than to me, or perhaps to no one in particular. "But to lose my God at the same time is more than I can take. Why should I want to get well? I haven't been able to pray since the accident. I guess I don't believe now that there's anybody running this world at all; or if there is, he certainly isn't the sort with whom I would care to be on friendly terms."

"Believe me," I told her again, "God did not either will or approve the accident that took the life of your boy. In fact, I am sure his tears have mingled with yours since the moment of that tragedy, and still do. The God I know needs the lives of young men like Ronnie to help build his kingdom. Instead of being set over against you in this tragedy, I am sure he has suffered serious loss along with you, has been very close to you through the tragedy, and shares deeply your sorrow."

Firing a look at me that all but seared with its intensity, she countered with, "Well, if God is so sorry about all this, why didn't he do something to prevent it? Are you meaning to tell me God is a weakling in his own world and no more able to prevent catastrophies like this than I am? Little help such a God would be to me if I did believe in him! If he regrets this incident as much as you indicate, why didn't he prevent it?"

"God certainly is not a weakling," I assured her, "and he is in complete control of his universe. He knew all about and could have prevented this accident, but he chose not to do so. If you had been in his place, bearing the responsibility he carries, I am sure you would have made the same decision he did."

"What do you mean by that?" she asked with growing interest. Sensing how very much was at stake in this exchange I proceeded slowly and very carefully. "As I see it, there were just three things God could have done to save Ronnie's life on that morning when he rode the manure spreader around your barn. First, God could have seized your son forcibly, and when he decided to make the trip could have said, "No! You are not going!" He could have overruled Ronnie's will and restrained him forcibly from doing what he had decided to do. But Mrs. Lowry, would you want to live in a world where persons have no will of their own, are not able to make their own decisions or carry out as best they can their own purposes? Would you like knowing that God, in order to avoid the possibility of our sinning and making mistakes due to ignorance, has deprived us of all initiative and freedom? Don't you realize these are the qualities that make us children of God instead of cogs in the wheel of a big machine? Such a deprivation might prevent all accidents, sufferings, and sins, but wouldn't it also rule out all achievements and virtues?"

She sat silently pondering this for a moment. I continued, "But there is a second way God could have saved Ronnie. When your son drove under that leaning silo and it began to fall under the pressure of a gust of wind, God could have picked it up and thrown it back over the other way. But again, would you feel we would be better off living in a world where the behavior of the physical world around us were as capricious as that, and could not be depended upon to be stable? Under such a circumstance wouldn't you be afraid even to pick up a book, like this one lying on your table, and let go of it? If only part of the time free objects traveled toward the center of the earth, the next time might they not very well fly up and hit you in the face? Don't you realize that a world of dependable, law-abiding physical objects constitutes the only workable environment in which we human beings possibly can build, advance, and develop?

After a reflective moment she said quietly, "You mentioned a third way God could have saved Ronnie, didn't you?"

"Yes," I answered. "And for you it might seem to be the big one. If you are able to agree that in the ideal management of our world both human free will and a law abiding physical environment might be wise and necessary, doesn't the thought still rush into your mind, 'But why couldn't God have made an exception in this case? Such a single, small intervention certainly would not have upset the structure of his whole creation; and knowing how much it would mean to me and our family, why couldn't he have intervened to help us? Would it be asking too much to expect a loving Father temporarily to set aside a rule of his household on an occasion when the very life of one of his children was at stake!'"

This I am sure constitutes the most pressing question in the minds of most of us in such a situation. We may agree completely with God's general plan for providing his children with freedom of will on the one hand, and a dependable physical world around us on the other. But why should he not keep a careful watch over the situation and his hand actively involved to protect and deliver us when some combination of circumstances threatens to injure or destroy us? Rules are undoubtedly important, but in a loving and well-ordered household, are they more important than the children?

At this point I reminded Mrs. Lowry of the New Testament declaration, "God shows no partiality" and is no respecter of persons *(Acts 10:34)*. Then I asked if she favored that arrangement. I said, "Suppose you were an all-loving heavenly parent and had decided on a policy of occasional intervention in the interest of your children. On what basis would you select the recipients of your favors? If you were to give special assistance to one child and deny it to another, would you help 'the good one' and ignore 'the bad one'? Jesus told us that the infinite love of our Father in heaven 'makes his sun to rise on the evil and on the good and sends his rain on the just and on the unjust.' If goodness were rewarded with heavenly protection and assistance, would it not cease to be virtue and become only shrewd policy which the smart operators would craftily adopt to their personal advantage? The author of the Book of Job argued this point effectively. After he had God point to Job in his comfort and affluence as an illustration of one who feared him and rejected evil, he had Satan answer, 'Does Job fear God for nought? Hast thou not put a hedge about him and his house and all that he has?' *(Job 1:8-10)* If you were God, would you have lifted Jesus off the cross? Do you really believe this would be a better world if God had done that, if he were a respecter of persons, made exceptions, showed partiality, and clearly operated with one set of rules for some and different standards for others?''

It was a full hour later when I left Mrs. Lowry's room. She was talking and asking questions freely at the close of our visit, and her doctor released her from the hospital three days later. At present she has her farm in good order and the children through high school. Unquestionably her recovery of physical and emotional health dated back from the moment when, with Margaret Fuller, she became able to cry out with intelligent conviction, ''I accept the universe!''

Over against this experience of hers I recall another circumstance that stands in sharp contrast to the attitude she achieved. Once while I was in the midst of oral examinations for my doctorate, a venerable scholar in the group began to press me vigorously regarding my Christian belief in a personal God who could be conceived as both omnipotent and benevolent. As the discussion continued I began to sense that his interest in the subject was more than academic because of the feeling he was registering. Suddenly I watched him settle back in his swivel chair, puff for a few seconds on his pipe, then turn on me almost furiously to ask, ''If you believe in a God both good and powerful, what would you say in response to this situation? My wife and I had one child, a boy of unusual brilliance and great potential. In the midst of his college career, however, we began to notice that his walking was being affected, his muscular coordination was breaking down, and he was no longer able to write legibly. An examination revealed that he was the victim of what was then diagnosed as dementia praecox. We had him in one hospital after another and spent all we had and more on his treatments. In spite of all that could be done, we were compelled

17

to watch him sink almost to the vegetable level before his death. A few months later his mother died of a broken heart. So here I am today, left alone with no family at all. What do you have to say to me in my circumstance, with respect to a universe presided over by an omnipotent and benevolent God?''

By this time the demeanor of the great old scholar had changed. He was leaning forward in his chair, his speech rapid, his attitude intense. I said to him, ''I have an answer to your question that to me is satisfactory. Let me convey it to you by relating a recent experience of mine as a parish minister when I was called into the north end of our city to conduct a funeral service that was being held in a small house. When I arrived, every room was crowded with relatives and friends. I learned that the deceased was a young husband and father in his late twenties who had been killed while coupling cars in his work as a railroad brakeman. The young wife and mother, with a year-old baby on her lap, could only stare at me appealing through eyes that were fixed and dry. She long since had cried herself to exhaustion. They were buying their small home and were full of thrilling plans that were both good and right, all of which now lay crushed before her like a shattered vase. The life purposes of this young man were almost totally unfulfilled; just when he was deeply loved and desperately needed, he was taken away. In the brief moment before the service began I was trying to determine what I could and should say to this silent, stunned, and confused circle of family and friends. Suddenly a telegram arrived, addressed to the young wife. A member of the family handed it to me to read to all present. It was from the superintendent of the railroad line. It told this stricken wife, ''I am so sorry because of the tragedy that has come into your life. Believe me it is not the intention of our company that a regrettable incident like your husband's death should ever occur. Instead, we do all we can to avoid such occasions of accident or injury, for it is our will that the railroad we operate should serve the happiness, usefulness, and convenience of all concerned. Occasionally, however, in spite of our best intentions and efforts, someone gets caught between the cars, and instead of being carried happily along to their destination, he is injured or killed, as was the case with your husband. In such a circumstance, all I can say to you and to the family is to ask you to be willing to stand within the shadow and help pay the price that so great a human service as a railroad can be possible.''

When I finished reading this message to those assembled, I said, ''I also bring you today a message—from God. His message is much the same. He is asking me to say to you, 'I am sorry this has happened. It is not my will that any of my children should suffer as you are suffering now. Indeed I have designed the world for the maximum happiness and usefulness of all my own who dwell in it. But occasionally someone gets caught between the laws by which the universe must be operated, and instead of being assisted, is hurt and injured as you are now. I can only ask you to believe that this is the best of all possible worlds, and plead with you to be willing to stand within the shadow and help pay the price that so great world as this could be possible.' ''

When I had concluded my story, I turned to the old scholar who had been listening intently throughout and said, ''With the tragic loss of your son and your wife, you have been called upon to pay a heavy price. There is, however, a great majority of life that is good, true, and beautiful. Some day the ravage of diseases, like the one that struck down your son, and of accidents like the one that took the young father from his family, will be eradicated, as increased knowledge of and cooperation with this universe and its laws delivers us from them. In the meantime, I believe you are asked to be willing to be among those who must stand within the shadow and help pay the price such a significant universe demands, heavy though its cost may be. Are you willing to do this?''

He fixed his eyes on me sharply for a long moment and then answered, sadly and bitterly, ''I am not! It's too high a price. It's not worth it.''

As we turned to another subject, I felt that for once I had witnessed an intelligent mind that was able to understand the issue clearly, look squarely into the face of God, and say, ''I disapprove of the way you run this world and I do not accept you or your universe as being either intelligent or friendly.'' His lonely lot, as a consequence of this attitude, was to live out his years in darkness, steeped in a bleak dreariness that was by far more tragic than anything he had previously experienced!

I will grant that without my firm belief in life after death, I myself frequently would find my own lips sealed. Like Job's three friends, I, too, would sit stunned and speechless before some of the situations that confront us. For example, when Margie first came to our church she was a high school girl few would notice. She was overweight, laughed so loudly she was an embarrassment to her friends, and lacked most of the accepted social graces. She had been raised in an orphans' home and now was farmed out with a family in our community to work her way through high school as a housemaid. God had endowed her, however, with one outstanding talent. She could sing alto with rich resonance, and had a natural gift for harmonizing that made her highly acceptable

19

in any singing group. After church on Sunday evenings we often would see the youth choir kids load into cars and take off for one of their homes or some other social rendezvous. But when they were all gone, Margie would be left standing on the sidewalk alone. She had such a sweet spirit that she would quietly go off home by herself without a complaint, and return next week as cheerful as ever.

Finally she married; but soon after the wedding she discovered her husband was an alcoholic. She had one baby after another. With little financial support or appreciation from her husband, she finally became unable to cope with the physical and emotional strain of her situation. After a brief and very painful illness, she lay in her casket at the age of thirty-two, cut down in mid-life without ever having had even a ghost of a chance at happiness or growth in the way her sensitive and kindly spirit would have desired.

As Christians, what do we have to say when we stand beside the casket at a funeral service like Margie's? Do we bow our heads submissively and intone, "It is the will of God, and we must accept it as such," or look into space, smell a flower, read a poem, sing a song, and hurry off to the cemetery?

This is not what I felt privileged and commissioned to do. At Margie's funeral I turned instead to all present—the father, his little children, and the assembled friends, and assured them with conviction, "This is not the will of God!" I made it clear from Matthew's recorded words of our Lord, "It is not the will of my Father who is in heaven that one of these little ones should perish!" *(18:14)* Instead we read in our Bible that it is our Father's will we should have approximately three-score and ten years in which to experience childhood, young man or womanhood, love, marriage and family, with all the joys and sorrows that attend these adventures; and in the process to be able to grow a soul firm enough to stand eternal in the heavens when the material forms of earth are knocked off by the incident of death. I made it very clear that Margie had had no semblance of a chance to experience most of those opportunities.

I thank God most perhaps for the next word I was able to speak as I stood by her casket, for I found myself saying, "My soul, sit thou a patient looker-on; judge not the play before the play is done. Her plot hath many changes; every day speaks a new scene; the last act crowns the play." [2] Without this conviction, my sense of life's justice in its dealing with individuals frequently would be so seriously violated that my courage for daily living would be undermined.

Margie in no way deserved, by the sweet-spirited response she made to life as it presented itself to her, the circumstances that came upon her. Neither do the petted and pampered ones all about us deserve the soft ride through life that so often is their lot. Some oriental religions have taught the doctrine of reincarnation as providing an answer to this dilemma, and it does indeed offer a satisfactory answer to many. By its dictates we are directed to look into the past to find explanation for the inequities of the present. When a good person like Margie suffers to the very end, while some self-centered, dishonest parasite on society continues to be coddled and deluged with good fortune, adherents to the belief in reincarnation have a ready answer. They assure us that Margie lived an evil existence in her former incarnation, while the playboy or society belle led an exemplary former life. This adds up to the conclusion that each now is reaping precisely the circumstance earned by his or her earlier behavior. This tenet of faith suggests one means of salvaging the justice of the universe to individuals now on stage in life's drama.

The reincarnation solution comes at a high price, however, for this hypothesis makes the status quo in any situation "the will of God"—precisely the way things should be. If the poor, diseased, ignorant, and enslaved of the world are in their present condition because it is fair and right that they should be there, then why should we bestir ourselves or make sacrifices to change their lot?

In sharp contrast is set the Christian doctrine of life after death. This view directs us to find the causes of human fortune, good or ill, in the inhumanity exhibited among persons both here and now and in the past, and exhorts us to begin immediately to relieve the miseries and wipe out these injustices. We are sustained in our effort by knowing it can be accomplished, for we have another whole act coming up in the play in case the task remains incomplete when the curtain is rung down on life's drama here. Historically this faith, in contrast to reincarnation, has stimulated social concern and action, and has resulted in the establishment of schools and hospitals as well as innumerable other institutions and efforts for aiding all kinds of suffering. It also has motivated the building of dams, the digging of irrigation ditches, and has triggered a multitude of efforts to subdue a recalcitrant nature and make "the kingdom of the world . . . become the kingdom of our Lord" *(Rev. 11:15).*

If you were to walk with me into a theatre during the second act of an average play, you well might find the hero bound and gagged, the heroine in the clutches of the villain, and foul injustice rampant on the stage. You conceivably might turn on

21

your heels and stalk toward the exit in disgust. I would pursue you, however, and urge, "Please don't go now. Stay around for a while. Don't you know there's another act coming up?"

If you should agree to return with me to our seats, frequently we would discover that in Act Three the hero extricates himself from his restraints and comes front and center in the nick of time. The heroine we see rescued, the villain hounded to his just punishment, and at curtain-fall, right and justice are prevailing. Just so, I believe unquestionably in the essential goodness and fairness of this universe! I know, however, even as Jesus did when he quoted Abraham in his story of the rich man and Lazarus, that more time is required than this earthly life provides in order to establish equity and to enable us to say, "now he is comforted here, and you are in anguish."

With respect to death in relation to the will of God, I also carry with me as part of my spiritual heritage another incident that marked radical alteration in my feeling and thinking and stands for me as a notable spiritual landmark. While I was a young minister in my late twenties I was asked to serve on a civic committee commissioned to survey two notorious "slum neighborhoods" in our community and help arouse public sentiment for their eradication. A competent social worker was serving as our guide.

The first event that impressed me took place while we were visiting a desperate mother in her ramshackle house on the east side of our city. In addition to the cold, the hunger, and the cramped quarters her family had to endure, she explained to us that since they had been unable to pay rent for two months, the landlord had shut off their only water supply, which consisted of a single outdoor faucet near their front porch. After hearing the woman's story, a dignified old minister in our group laid his hand on her shoulder and in a stained-glass tone said solemnly, "Now sister! You just have faith in the Lord, and everything will come out all right." The distraught woman looked up at him respectfully, nodded her head slightly, and then drawing herself up straight she shouted, "Yes sir, Brother! That's all right. But what we need now is WATER!" Never since that day have I needed further evidence that although "man shall not live by bread alone," it is equally true that he cannot live without bread. In fact, the basic physical needs of the average person take priority over spiritual concerns, in chronological sequence even if not always on the scale of value judgments.

Then came this other crucial scene that I hope I may be able here adequately to record, in order that its spiritual overtones may be communicated. As we continued our housing tour, we suddenly encountered a funeral procession winding its way into a barren little chapel a block away. Our matronly guide asked if we would like to take a few minutes to attend the service with her. On our way there she explained to us that she knew and loved the deceased, and that Nellie Mae had been one of her most responsive clients for several years. She was a hardworking mother of ten children, had borne one every year since she had married, and was so run down physically that her doctor had warned her when the tenth baby came not to have any more. He referred her to the newly established "Mother's Health Clinic" in our city for contraceptive advice and equipment. Our guide, her social worker, assisted her with advice and baby care, and for three years she had gone without a pregnancy. Her health improved, her spirits rose, and the family was doing quite well. Then one day a committee of women from this little chapel where the family attended Sunday school and church visited Nellie Mae. They had heard of her visits to the Mother's Health Clinic, and they told her the entire congregation including the pastor was shocked by what she was doing. They explained that she would have to discontinue the trips and abandon her contraceptive practices or be ejected from the church membership and be liable to an eternity in hell. They explained to her that she was defeating the will of God by what she was doing and that such conduct could not be tolerated by their congregation. Nellie Mae, a person of good heart and will, certainly did not want to defeat the will of God, so fearfully but obediently she complied with the committee's instructions.

Our narrator concluded as we reached the church door, "By the time I made my next visit to her home she was pregnant, and when her eleventh baby was born three days ago she died in delivery. This is her funeral service we are now going to attend."

The scene on the front pew was not easy to forget. The oldest daughter, who was in junior high school, sat at one end of the seat and the broken-hearted husband and father at the other. He really was a kindly man of elemental nature, a hard worker who loved his family and would not for the world have hurt Nellie Mae. As life presented itself to this simple couple, however, their very love for each other and its normal expression was the fact that resulted in her death and their separation. Between the thirteen-year-old girl and her father sat the nine other children, the new baby being cared for at home by a neighbor.

Then came the minister's funeral sermon. It was primarily an evangelistic exhortation, delivered with evident dramatics while this occasion provided him a larger audience than he usually was able to command. Accompanying his homiletic effort were personal references made to "good Sister Nellie Mae." He extolled her virtues and assured the family and friends that "God needed the brightness and sweetness of this lovely flower in his garden of love." He told her family that it was entirely right and good that he who made her should also have the right to take her, whenever in his wisdom he considered it best to do so. He repeatedly assured his listeners, "This is the will of God and we must accept it as such. We may have difficulty seeing it now, but this is because we see through a glass darkly." Then the choir, consisting of some of the same women who composed the committee that visited Nellie Mae a year before, sang "Some Day We'll Understand," and the service was over.

That funeral may have concluded with the benediction for most in attendance, but for me it has been echoing back and forth through the caves of my thought and feeling to this very day. Each time I project myself back into that little chapel, hear the pious voice of Nellie Mae's preacher, and recall the speech the church committee made to her in her home, all the bells in my belfry ring out in protest.

Did that minister say he had difficulty in seeing why God had taken Nellie Mae from her family? No wonder he was unable to see it, because it never happened! He was looking in the wrong place for the cause of the death of that young mother, who so desperately was needed for years to come to be with and help rear her family. Actually she was the tragic victim of a group of obscurantist, misguided, pseudo-religious moralists who had "a zeal for God, but it is not enlightened" *(Rom. 10:2)*.

Did they say, when Nellie Mae was trying in her marriage intelligently to control the creative forces of childbirth, that she was "defeating the will of God"? What is the assumption here? Do we consider that the will of God is best accomplished when our intelligence and will is prevented from participating in the issue? This certainly is not the way God's will is done elsewhere in his world. Our very earliest biblical references assure us that from the dawn of creation God has said to man, with reference to the facts and forces of life he has placed within our reach, "subdue them and have dominion over them" *(See Gen. 1)*.

When God wants to grow a garden of good vegetables for the sustenance of his children, does he say to us, "Don't inject your intelligence and effort into this project, lest you defeat my will"? As a matter of fact it is essential, after first consulting God about the wisdom of the project, that we should bring the plot under our own control, plant the cabbages here, the beans there, hoe out the weeds everywhere, cultivate, fertilize, and water as best our knowledge and scientifically designed tools make possible. When we, through this kind of cooperation with God have the project flourishing, we again should subject our will to our Father's to determine the disposition of the harvest. It is after this order that the will of God is done to best advantage in the affairs of people, and throughout the procedure we surely will be held morally responsible for using every device our ingenuity can conceive to accomplish the desired ends to the best advantage. If a sin is involved, it is not nearly as likely to consist in the kind of tools we employ as in the use we make of the crop after it has been harvested. If we disregard the hungry about us and sell our produce entirely to add to our pleasure or feed our vanity, God will surely hold us to strict account for our improper disposition of the increase, not for the techniques by which it was produced.

Just so, if Nellie Mae had utilized her intelligent control and limitation of childbearing in her family merely in order to spend idle hours in illicit or extra-marital licentiousness, God's displeasure would have been assured. It would have been incurred, however, not because of the fact or method of her contraceptive procedures, but by the purposes to which she employed them.

This episode has stood out in my life as a significant monument, and has enabled me often since to say with conviction as I have stood beside the casket of some counterpart of Nellie Mae, "This is not the will of God!" I am even more grateful that I also am able to say as I contemplate the many frustrated lives tragedy has plagued and overtaken, "My soul, sit thou a patient looker-on, judge not the play before the play is done."

# Chapter 3

## If Only I Could Believe!

Now that we have come this far regarding belief in life after death, is there perhaps one of you who has dropped the book for a moment, stared into space wistfully, and said, "I wish I could believe that"? One scholarly man of renown in his professional field told me recently, "I sincerely wish I could share the faith you have just expressed. What a comfort and joy it would provide me. But I seem totally unable to believe these things you seem to accept so wholeheartedly."

Let me make it clear that I hold no illusions about the ground on which these convictions rest with respect to immortality. They are rooted in faith, not in proofs or evidence that would stand indisputably in a court of scientific inquiry. I do not submit this statement, however, without first having made every effort possible to discover whether proofs and evidences are available. For my doctor's dissertation in philosophy, I conducted research over a period of several years on the theme, "The Ethical Significance of Abnormal Experiences." In the course of this quest I devoted much time to examination of purported evidences of survival. I became acquainted with Dr. Elwood Worcester, founder of the Emanuel Movement in Boston, and carried on correspondence with him during the period when he became convinced that in sittings with creditable mediums he had secured facts that could not possibly be known by any living person. I also acquainted myself with the findings of the American Society for Psychical Research, and with several outstanding scholars across our nation who have conducted experiments and done invaluable research in this field. I personally made numerous visits to mediums and psychics, participated in seances of all the types accredited by the most trustworthy advisors, and received much stimulating and revealing information as reward for my effort. But as far as relevance to the subject matter of this book is concerned, I can only state that at no time did I encounter any experience I honestly felt carried sufficient weight to be considered scientific evidence or proof of survival. In all the "messages" or "appearances" I encountered, when I applied the logical principle of "Occam's razor," I concluded that the phenomenon confronting me could be explained more readily by some other and simpler hypothesis than the "spirit manifestation" the medium insisted was its source.

The same is true with respect to philosophical or theological arguments that have been set forth through the years in purported substantiation of life after death. They frequently are very interesting and helpful. They may indeed tend to throw the balance of the scale of thought in favor of faith in immortality, but in no instance do they constitute irrefutable proof of it. Therefore, I conclude that if any of us is ever to hold a positive conviction concerning life after death that will support and sustain in the manner I have been presenting in the previous chapters of this book, it admittedly must rest on faith.

At this point in my thinking it was the grand old American scholar William James who came to my aid during my college days. I had about come to the conclusion that agnosticism was the only honest attitude an intelligent mind could adopt when confronted with mutually exclusive alternatives of belief. But I could secure no compelling evidence in support or refutation of either. I conceived this to be precisely the situation regarding life after death, for I felt I would be on ground just as indefensible if I avowed disbelief in it as if I embraced it. I therefore was preparing to settle for the dictum of the agnostic, "I don't know," which unfortunately seems always to assure us creditable standing in academic circles. I even felt a measure of cultural superiority in my detachment and rejoiced that this position could not involve me in the possible embarrassment of being proved wrong, or leave me open to charges of being unscholarly in my stance.

Then I became acquainted with William James, the practical genius who convinced the thinking world that after all arguments are over and the research efforts are concluded, the need of human individuals with their loves and longings still has a report to submit that cannot be ignored. I was stirred to the depths as James pointed out that for most of us suspended judgment is a tolerable frame of mind only with respect to proposals about which we do not need to do anything or take any action. If you raise before me the question, "How many rings are there around the planet Saturn?" I very well may shrug my shoulders, lapse comfortably into an attitude of nonchalance, and dismiss your question with the response, "I don't know or care." Why can I do this? Because I have no intention of doing anything about Saturn's rings, and therefore have no need for acquiring a conviction regarding their number. But James went on to point out that when, on the contrary, the question raised involves a moral issue of practical importance to me, and is one in regard to which I feel compelled to act as if one or the other of the proposals is true, then suspended judgment becomes no longer tolerable, either emotionally or rationally. By practical necessity I am smoked out of my detachment as a balcony sitter, and feel compelled to roll up my sleeves and get involved in the arena of life and decision.

When the full impact of Professor James' line of reasoning had registered convincingly on my mind, I swung its searchlight on my agnosticism regarding the Christian doctrine of life after death. I realized that for me this issue constituted just such a moral issue as he had been discussing because considerations of both my emotions and will were deeply involved here. It was clear to me that the practical course of my life would be differently ordered if I believed all my friends and loved ones would live on with me after death. I would certainly do many things differently than would be the case if I rejected such a faith and considered the grave my final goal. I reached the conclusion, therefore, that I was under real compulsion to make up my mind on this matter.

Then suddenly I received a second impetus to get out of the balcony and into the arena of this subject. I discovered my emotions were screaming at me. By now I had lived longer, had attached myself by bonds of affection to other persons more deeply, and had lost heavily from among those I loved most dearly. Previously I had convinced myself that I could be nonchalant about my own future. I reasoned, "One world at a time. If I wake up after the sleep of death, I'll try to adjust myself to whatever environment I find myself in there just as I have done here. But if in death I perish, I perish, so I'm not much concerned about whether I'm 'to be or not to be.'" Then came the abrupt shock of looking suddenly into the waxen features of someone I loved more than my own life, and about whose future in togetherness with me I discovered I just could not be unconcerned. Could I view that beloved face and say with a shrug as I turned from the casket, "Well, I may see you again, and I may not. I can't say that it matters"? Indeed it did matter to me—desperately—and suddenly all the heartstrings of my soul were vibrating violently under the winds of love's separation. My emotions were pleading in unison with my will for a decision with respect to the conviction I should hold regarding life beyond the grave.

But what decision could I honestly make, when admittedly no

real evidence was available either for or against the proposal? Again Professor James came to my aid. In a booklet bearing the title *The Will to Believe,* he furnished the crowning point for my arch of logical thinking. I heard this great scholar saying to me in effect,

> This is a moral universe in which the belief that is true works out the best, in the long run and on the whole, when subjected to the laboratory tests of practical living. Therefore, if you find it necessary to make a decision in any instance where factual evidence is not available, either in support or refutation of a hypothesis, choose the proposal that works out the best in the crucible of your own life experience, and it is more likely to be true.

Professor James at this point impressed me deeply because I, too, believe this to be a moral universe, and therefore this line of reasoning appears valid and his pragmatic test for truth acceptable.

This brings me to my answer for any one of you who finds yourself saying, "If only I could believe in life after death!" This kind of faith is not a mysterious gift which life bestows on some individuals and withholds from others. By my experience and observation, faith at its best is an achievement, the product of scientific observation culminating in an act of will, which then is sustained by disciplined effort and practical use. Sam Jones, the homespun evangelist of our grandfathers' generation, told a story of a man he found in a snow-covered woods on a bitter-cold day. He was leaning on his axe and shivering beside a tree marked for felling. When Rev. Jones asked him what he was doing, the reply came back, "I'm getting ready to cut down this tree. I remember, though, that every man I've ever seen cutting down a tree was sweating, so I'm waiting for the sweat to come; and when it does I'll start chopping!"

Let me present the same idea in another illustration. Let us suppose you would like to become a blacksmith. But you discover with your first attempt that the great hammer and the heavy tongs tire you completely out, and you have to lay them down. What do you do now? Do you remember that every blacksmith you ever knew had a great set of arm and chest muscles? Do you recall, "The smith a mighty man is he with large and sinewy hands. And the muscles of his brawny arms are strong as iron bands"?[3] If you, therefore, conclude that being a good blacksmith requires having strong arm and chest muscles, you will be entirely right. But how do you go about getting them? Should you earnestly desire them? Should you pray for them? By all means you should do both. Experience has taught me, however, that God hears and answers only such prayers as originate in sincere thought, become articulate in intelligible words, and then finally are implemented in the most appropriate action possible to us under our circumstances. You may desire and pray at length for the muscles you will need for your proposed career, but it will only be when you begin expressing those wishes and prayers by picking up the hammer and swinging it as best you can with your present equipment that God will say, "Now I can hear you." Only then will he begin undergirding your petitions with the callouses, muscles, and skills required to be a blacksmith.

Faith, according to my experience, is acquired in precisely this same fashion. With respect to life after death, I first exercised my "will to believe." I concluded definitely that the materialism and this-worldliness set forth in the Book of Ecclesiastes does not work out well as a basis for courageous and significant living. Listen to that author's reflections relative to life and death: "A living dog is better than a dead lion. For the living know that they will die, but the dead know nothing, and they have no more reward; but the memory of them is lost. . . . Go, eat your bread with enjoyment, and drink your wine with a merry heart. . . . Whatever your hand finds to do, do it with your might; for there is no work or thought or knowledge or wisdom in Sheol, to which you are going" *(Eccles. 9:4f)*. Contrast this point of view with that of the apostle Paul: "I tell you a mystery. We shall not all sleep, but we shall all be changed. . . . The dead will be raised imperishable. . . . Then shall come to pass the saying that is written: 'Death is swallowed up in victory. O death, where is thy victory? O death, where is thy sting?' . . . Thanks be to God, who gives us the victory through our Lord Jesus Christ" *(1 Cor. 15:51f)*.

It seems completely convincing to me that this latter conviction works out better for daily living in the long run and on the whole. It sustains happy and useful living through the varied circumstances life often brings, and often lifts the believer to his most glorious heights of joy and peace at the approach of death. The picture Ecclesiastes presents leaves our human lives creeping feebly and sadly toward dissolution and decay in a cold, dark grave. Younger persons may be able to espouse the atheistic, materialistic, and hedonistic philosophies with bravado, but when the universal experience of old age moves in, the honest mind is almost compelled to wail with an old man of eighty-five years, "Myself when young could sit down quite content with 'the jug of wine, the loaf of bread, and thee.' But now the jug is empty, the bread is eaten, and she died many years ago.'' Any belief I will adopt must stand the test of living experience in the long run and on the whole, in age as well as in youth. It seems quite conclusive to me that Paul spoke accurately when he exclaimed, ''If in this life we who are in Christ have only hope, we are of all men most to be pitied'' *(1 Cor. 15:19).*

How gloriously the Christian hope and interpretation of life after death sustains a healthy spirit for enthusiastic living, not only in youth and old age but on through them both. A prominent surgeon in our city told me recently of a critical situation he faced in honesty with an old man in his eighties who required surgery, but had no more than a 10% chance of coming through the ordeal and recovering. When advised of the situation confronting him, the kindly old patient hesitated not at all in choosing the operation. He made it clear that he wanted very much to live, and also that he accepted the risks of his predicament calmly. Just before the attendants began administering the anesthetic, the surgeon went in for a brief visit with his old friend and found him reading his Bible absorbingly—apparently unconcerned about his approaching ordeal.

The doctor asked, ''How can you read like that at a time like this?'' With a calm smile the old man answered, ''Well, you see the author of this book I'm reading is an old friend of mine. Hosea lost his wife. He yearned for her and wept long and sadly over her departure. I lost my wife several years ago, and many evenings Hosea and I have shared our tears and feelings in close friendship. It just occurred to me that I may meet this old friend of mine face to face before this day is over, and I thought I'd like to refresh my memory of his book before I talk with him about it.''

I visited recently the remains of the ancient Mamertine Prison in Rome, that foul and dismal old cistern where Paul was confined during his last hours. I also sat alone in the crypt beneath the Church of John and Paul where a small plaque bears the inscription, ''At this spot Paul was beheaded.'' I recalled the imprisonments, the beatings, the hardships and trials that Paul endured for his Lord. I heard Paul dictating as he did so often in his imprisonments, even as the headsman's axe was a stark reality over his head: ''I have fought the good fight, I have finished the race, I have kept the faith. Henceforth. . . . ''

But shouldn't we interrupt him at this point to say, ''Just a minute, Paul. Aren't you forgetting your situation? Don't you realize this could well be the end for you? You have had a remarkable past indeed, but isn't the word *henceforth* a bit presumptuous under your present circumstance?''

Now watch the smile break over his glowing face as he asks, ''Are you referring to the possibility of death? That would only mark the end of Act I in my life drama. 'For to me to live is Christ, and to die is gain. . . . Henceforth there is laid up for me the crown of righteousness, which the Lord, the righteous judge, will award to me on that Day, and not only to me but also to all who have loved his appearing' '' *(Phil. 1:21; 2 Tim. 4:8).* Could we hope to witness a finer triumph than this over a more difficult circumstance? Could we ask of a belief that it pass a more severe test more conclusively than to provide such a wealth of joy, courage, and hope for a condemned prisoner in a cold dungeon and make it his most glorious hour?

Dr. Lyman Abbott, the great English preacher, left us a similar witness of the ability of this tenet of the Christian faith to sustain an eager attitude to the last breath. In his final hours he said,

> I look forward to the great adventure . . . with awe, but not with apprehension. I enjoy my work, my home, my friends, my life. I shall be sorry to part with them. But always I have stood in the bow looking forward with hopeful anticipation to the life before me. When the time comes for my embarkation, and the ropes are cast off and I put out to sea, I think I shall still be standing in the bow and still looking forward with eager curiosity and glad hopefulness to the new world to which the unknown voyage will bring me.[4]

You who are hesitant about believing in life after death as taught by our Christian faith: There is no one who can prove survival and personal immortality to you, and most certainly there is not one shred of evidence anyone can present you that will disprove it. You must make a decision and exercise your ''will to believe.'' I realize that in our western culture we live in a climate conducive to materialistic attitudes. The inductive method, based on sense observations by use of the test tube and magnifying lens, holds sway all around us, and the influence of scientific interest penetrates and permeates us. Rufus Jones, the famed Haverford Quaker and scholarly professor, wrote,

> One striking effect of ''naturalism'' on the modern mind has been the disappearance, or at least the weakened hold, of faith in immortal life. No one quite knows in a particular case why his faith in a future life oozed away and vanished.

It has not usually been dislodged by argument, certainly not by any proofs. *Eternal* life somehow just does not seem to fit the kind of world one finds left to him by current interpretations. The hope of a great future life has grown dim, the expectation of it has waned away. . . . It no longer figures as an inward resource in a day of sorrow and frustration. . . . The modern person has grown "weak in futurity." The "spell of eternity" is not for him. It may well be surmised that no other change of outlook has so profoundly affected the life and thought of this generation as has this blight of temporality that has thus fallen upon it. If a new day of faith is to dawn for this age it will almost certainly have as its morning star a new-born expectancy in the conservation of the supreme value of personal life.[5]

I thank God for the day when I made up my mind and exercised my will wholeheartedly to accept the Christian conviction regarding personal immortality as taught by New Testament scripture. As the years passed I have had increased occasion to utilize this faith and to lean on it as a strong inner resource. In consequence it has grown to such a degree of certainty in my life that I can say without shadow of doubt, "I know in whom I believe . . . for me to die is gain!" This same achievement can be yours also if you really want it and are willing to exercise the effort to win it. If you are "tender-minded," as William James expressed it, you will find the task fairly easy, but you will also be inclined to hold it more lightly and lose it more readily. If on the other hand you are "tough-minded," as has been my own situation, and find it necessary to fight vigorously for every conclusion you reach and each conviction you hold, you will discover that when you do achieve your mind-set, it will have deep roots and will stand the strain of any storms or strains to which it may be subjected.

After having stated my belief in life after death so positively, let me hasten to add that my mind is not closed on this subject, or on any other. The conviction I hold, however, is solid and firm. William James gave me another monumental assist at this point. In another of his essays bearing the title "The Practical Absolute," I heard him saying to me that in matters of practical or moral significance, it is impossible to live with enthusiasm and effectiveness if the best you can say is, "This is what I believe today, but I don't know what I may think about it tomorrow." Therefore, when you reach the best conclusion you can achieve in light of all the present thought available, nail down that conviction firmly in your mind and act upon it as if it were the absolute truth.

For you, let it become your "practical absolute," but always keep yourself alert and receptive to the acquisition of any new truth anyone can present that has bearing on the subject. Be prepared to move to a new position if creditable evidence warrants your doing so. Then make that new position your practical absolute, and once more throw into gear your assent and action in complete confidence. Only in this manner can you ever live with energy and enthusiasm. Suspended judgment provides no proper motivation for effective living.

This conviction is basic to my philosophy of life, not only with respect to belief in life after death but to many other of the beliefs and attitudes I hold. It has sustained me long and well in eager involvement with significant living. I commend it wholeheartedly to all of you who may read this, and particularly to you who have been saying, "If only I could believe that!"

# Chapter 4

## What Will It Be Like on the Other Side?

Hardly anyone who thinks much about life after death will fail to come up against the question, "What will life in the spirit following loss of the body be like?" I am certain that for many of us, failure to reach a satisfactory answer to this question constitutes a barrier to our faith in immortality. This is why I believe it important to share some conclusions I have reached in this regard. My own tough-mindedness requires that any belief to which I give assent must (1) be reasonable, (2) be in accord with all known facts, and (3) be conducive to better living. As Dr. Harry Emerson Fosdick once expressed it, "Two questions today face every proposition and custom of religion. First, is it intelligently defensible? Second, does it contribute to man's abundant life?" [6] In search of satisfactory answers to the question of what it will be like on the other side, I have reached some conclusions that for me have relieved the strain on my faith and made my belief in life after death not only acceptable to me, but stimulating and helpful. I make no claims for these points of view beyond stating that they pass the three tests I have cited above quite satisfactorily, and furthermore have been very useful to me in rounding out a workable life philosophy. It is in the hope that they may assist you also that I submit them here.

Recently a minister in a New York church reported a stroll he took in the woods with his small boy. Any time spent with this little chap involved listening to a running commentary, and as the father reports it, "The conversation unrolled like a skein of yarn, leading the two of us down a long and torturous corridor." Suddenly the little chap was heard asking,

"Daddy, why are those lines in your face?"

"O, I don't know. Because I'm getting old, I guess."

"But Daddy, does everybody get lines and grow old?"

"Well Son, they all grow old, and usually they get lines."

"Daddy, will I get lines in my face, and will I get old?"

"As I said before, everybody gets old, and that includes you."

"Daddy . . . what happens after you get old?"

"Well, in time you . . . well, you die."

"Do you think you'll die, Daddy?"

"O yes, everybody dies. And that includes me." (A long silence)

"Daddy . . . will I get lines, and will I die?"

"Yes, son, you will get lines, and you will die."

Suddenly that little countenance was stricken with fear, almost with terror as the boy looked up into his father's face. Fortunately for that child, he had a father who was able to respond sensitively and quickly. The young minister tells us, "I knew the hour had come. The fact of death had suddenly taken shape in the mind of a five-year-old and must be dealt with promptly. I smiled down at him warmly and said, 'But don't be too concerned about that, son. Come over here, and let's sit together on this log while I tell you the rest of the story.'"

How very important it is that there is more to the story, and how fortunate for one little boy that his father had something significant to say to him the first time the question of death arose in his mind! Many people do not have "the rest of the story" clearly in focus, even in their own later years; and it becomes extremely difficult to find their own spiritual support, to say nothing of helping others.

A generation ago, a boy by the name of John Todd was born in Vermont. When John was only six years old, his parents died. The children in the family were parceled out among the relatives, and John was sent to a kind-hearted aunt who lived in a village many miles away. Years later he entered Yale University, and after graduating from there he studied for the ministry. In the course of time he became one of the most renowned preachers of New England. Then one day he received a letter from his dear old aunt. Her doctor had told her she was the victim of an incurable disease and that her death was inevitable and imminent. In apparent distress of mind she wrote to her nephew:

"Tell me about death! What do I have to look forward to? Is it something to fear?" Here was an earnest person seeking an answer to the very question we have before us, and John Todd's reply to his beloved old aunt still is as stimulating and inspiring as the day she received it:

"It is now thirty-five years since I, a little boy of six, was left alone in the world. You sent me word you would give me a home and be a kind mother to me. I remember vividly the day I made the long journey from my former home to yours.

"I still recall my disappointment when I learned that instead of coming for me yourself, you had sent Caesar to bring me. Perched high on your horse and clinging tightly to Caesar, I remember my tears and anxiety as I rode toward my new home. Night fell before we finished the journey, and as the darkness deepened I began to be afraid.

'Do you think she'll go to bed before we get there,' I asked Caesar anxiously. 'Oh no,' he replied, 'she'll stay up for you all right. And when we get out of these woods right up ahead, you'll see her candle in the window sure enough.'

"Presently we rode out into a clearing, and there as Caesar had promised I saw the friendly light of welcome. I remember well how you were waiting at the door, and how you put your arms around me and lifted me, a tired and bewildered little boy, down from the horse. There was a bright fire on your hearth and a warm supper on your table. After we had eaten you took me up to my room, heard me say my prayers, and then sat close beside me until I dropped off to sleep.

"You probably are wondering why I am recalling all these things to your mind just now. Well, some day very soon now God will send for you to take you to your new home. Don't be afraid of the summons, the strange journey, or the Messenger Death. Believe me, at the end of the road you will find your Father waiting with open arms. A candle will be burning in the window, and a warm welcome in his care and keeping will be awaiting you. God can be trusted, Auntie, to be just as kind and loving to you as you were to me thirty-five years ago."

This offers, I realize, only one person's general response to the question, "What will it be like on the other side?" But I am convinced that it is along the path of the idea presented here that the more detailed answers will come.

I was deeply moved recently to hear a prominent surgeon relate the following more specific experience. He was visiting a patient of advanced years in his hospital room. Suddenly the older man turned to his doctor and asked pointedly, "Tell me the truth. Am I going to pull out of this?"

After a thoughtful pause this competent physician answered, "I really don't know. You've asked me to be honest with you and I will be. If you have another attack like the one that brought you in here, you will not survive it; and there is no way to tell whether that attack will come in six months or before you leave this hospital."

In quite evident fear the patient leaned forward and asked intently, "What is it like on the other side, Doctor? I suddenly realize I need to know, and I've never given this sort of thing a moment's consideration in my life.''

With a quiet smile this Christian physician responded, ''I don't know either.'' Then, while he paused to ask himself what he could say in answer to so earnest a question, he suddenly heard a scratching at the door. He opened it, and to his surprise and embarrassment saw his dog leap into the room and begin jumping on him in uncontrollable joy. Turning to the patient, the doctor said with sudden inspiration:

''Do you understand that this is my dog? Somehow he got out of my car and has trailed me through the hospital to this door. He has never been in this room before. He knew nothing whatever of what it is like in here, with one exception. He knew his master was in here. That was enough, and when the door opened he came right through it with no trace of reluctance or fear. Indeed, he leaped into this strange room with eagerness and anticipation because of the love and trust in his relationship with me. This indicates the answer I would give to your question about what it's like on the other side of death. I don't know! But I do know that my Master is there, and so are a lot of other grand people I have loved in my life. When the door opens for me, I'll walk right through and not be a bit afraid.''

As the doctor gathered the dog in his arms and headed back for his car, the old man in the hospital bed settled back on his pillow. The relaxed lines in his face gave evidence that a simple suggestion based on a homely drama enacted in his room had brought help and hope to his troubled spirit in an hour of need.

There is one belief, concerning what it will be like on the other side of death, to which I must hold firmly. It is the assurance that we will have our memory with us intact, will recall all we have known here, and will recognize our friends (and enemies) and be recognized by them. Any conception of immortality I may entertain that does not provide for a continuation of my consciousness in uninterrupted progression from my experience here is for me not worth holding, will not provide the strength and comfort I need to derive from such a faith, and does not seem to be in accord with the teachings of Jesus and the New Testament on the subject. If my memory is not preserved in the life I experience after death, in no real sense will ''I'' be there.

For many this is a sobering thought, for if our minds and spirits are now so hampered by fears, suspicions, resentments, and guilt that we cannot enjoy a single hour of peace and happiness, why do we think we will be able to do any better ''over there'' than we are doing here? Do we believe that the incident of death will suddenly work some miracle of transformation in us that will convert miserable sinners into glorious saints "in a moment, in the twinkling of an eye"? Surely we should be mature enough by now to know that the character flaws and defects we have allowed to lay hold on us must be dissolved and removed from our lives by the acceptance of the forgiving love of God, and that by no other means can we know real life anywhere. The sooner, then, that we get at the task of becoming reconciled to right relationships with our Father and with his other children, particularly the nearest others in our life, the better it will be for us. Death surely is not going to wave any magic wand over us and turn our "sow's ear into a silk purse," as our rural fathers might have expressed it.

As a consequence of this, what a bitter disappointment many people are going to experience! They often moan and sigh their way through this "vale of tears" in the fond hope that some day they will get to "Heaven," which they expect to be so lovely and beautiful that they can be happy in spite of what they are. I am convinced that those will make the best and happiest go of life beyond death who make the best and happiest go of life here. In the world after death, the same Father-God is in charge; and his children must work out relationships under the same set of rules he has ordained for us in this life. Perhaps this is the point of view that gives real meaning to Paul's exhortation to the Corinthians, "now is the day of salvation!" (2 Cor. 6:2)

But did Jesus teach "heavenly recognition," as our fathers designated it, and the retention of individual personality, including memory, in the life to come? He certainly seems to have done so, and most directly in Luke 16, with the story of the rich man in the palace and Lazarus lying at his gate. When these two men died, we read that Lazarus was immediately at home in "Abraham's bosom" while the rich man found himself "in Hades, being in torment." The point at which this story becomes meaningful to us in regard to the question we are considering is when Dives calls out a greeting to Father Abraham, whom he sees and recognizes.

What kind of body do we have in the life after death? According to both Jesus (in the story just related) and Paul (in 2 Cor. 5:1-4 and 1 Cor. 15:35-38) it certainly will be as adequate to whatever environment we find ourselves in there, as this one is to our present circumstances; and it will be so similar to our present body that, as the exchange between Dives and Father Abraham shows, it will be readily recognizable. "And what you sow is not the body which is to be. . . . But God gives it a body as he has chosen." Commenting on these words from Paul, L. Harold DeWolf says:

> The vast resourcefulness of God, evident in the variety of His visible creation, shows us that He can provide a body suited to each kind of existence which He purposes to sustain (1 Cor. 15:39-40). Paul does not tell us much about the "spiritual body" which is to be. And with good reason. We can no more anticipate the kind of body with which we shall be "further clothed" after death than we could have our present mental ability before entering our present life. But the God who did anticipate and create this present "earthly tent" can be trusted to provide also that "house not made with hands" which is to serve our future needs. We do not know the future. But we know Him and so we are content.[7]

Rufus Moseley left us a priceless comment at this point. Following one of his addresses at a Camp Farthest Out, someone came to him and asked, "What will our bodies be like over there, Brother Rufus?" With a twinkle in his eye, the grand old saint answered, "Well, I figure it'll be like this. Every once in a while somebody gives me a new suit of clothes. When I first put that suit on it looks fashionable and stylish, but by about the third day it begins to take on that Moseley look! I figure that's the way it'll be with whatever body the Lord gives me when I get over on that other side. It may be a little strange at first, but by about the third day it'll begin to take on that Moseley look."

Not only did Jesus indicate the retention of our memories in the life after death by assuring us that the rich man saw and recognized Lazarus, but he furthermore has Father Abraham call out to Dives in his torment, "Son, remember that you in your lifetime received your good things, and Lazarus in like manner evil things, but now he is comforted here, and you are in anguish." This makes it quite clear to me that over there we readily will recall the happenings of this lifetime. In this story Jesus seems to be telling us that we will have bodies over there that will look enough like these we now possess to make them clearly recognizable, that we will know each other on that far side of death, and that our memories will be with us intact.

From this same parable it would appear also that no long period of time will intervene between our death and our awakening in the spirit world. Many of our fathers believed in "soul-sleeping," and taught that we will pass at death into a deep sleep from which we shall not awaken until the trumpet sounds for "Judgment

Day,'' perhaps thousands of years in the future. Jesus seems to repudiate this concept, for when the rich man was unable to secure valet service from Lazarus to ease his tortures in the flames of hell, he begged Abraham, "Then . . . send him to my father's house, for I have five brothers, so that he may warn them, lest they also come into this place of torment." This conversation could not have taken place centuries later. It evidently occurred the next day, or soon thereafter, for those five brothers were still living and in position to profit by his proposed warning.

Still one more vital lesson is inherent in this parable. I refer now to the "great chasm" that Abraham spoke of as being fixed "between us and you . . . in order that those who would pass from here to you may not be able, and none may cross from there to us." I clearly can observe deep furrows being plowed between us here in our everyday human relationships that indicate how true our Lord's description may be of unsurpassable canyons separating us by the time we are over there. Have you ever had the experience of attending a reunion back home in the little farm or village community where you were born? Many of the native residents there have lived quite simple and uneventful lives in the years since you left. It is good to see them, and for the first five minutes you exchange happy greetings and share nostalgic reminiscences. But then you suddenly discover you have run out of anything to talk about. The moment the conversation turns to religious, social, or political issues—things that matter most in your life—you cease to communicate. Even worse, you may discover your deepest and most precious convictions arouse in them icy stares and wounded feelings that remind you how far you have strayed from the narrow confines of your early and restricted moorings. You probably are forced very quickly to realize that between you and those childhood associates of yours "a great chasm is fixed which no one can cross."

It is much more tragic when this yawning gulf develops between a husband and wife, living side by side for decades in the same house. I shall never forget the indelible impression made on me during my early ministry by Mrs. O'Neil. She was very faithful to her church and always came alone with her children. One morning I was called by the family to come to her bedside quickly. I learned when I arrived that she was in the final stages of a terminal illness, the primary factor of which was venereal disease that had been brought home to her by an alcoholic husband. She asked the family to leave us alone. Her first words were, "I know I'm going to die, but I don't want to die. There is something I would like before I go. I want to work with young people. I realize I will never get to do it, so I want to send a message to them through you. Tell them, 'Be careful of a hasty marriage.' Then she described the ordeals she had gone through in her marital experience, a union that had been contracted hastily between a 17-year-old, naive country girl, and a flashy young man from the city who promised her lavender and roses. After picturing for me how hard she had tried to build a good home and a happy marriage with him, and how ruthlessly he had walked roughshod over her tenderest feelings and highest aspirations, she added, "We have lived our twenty years of married life in two separate circles that never once touched. The things I loved, like church, lectures, concerts, or schooling, he scoffed at and rejected. The things and places he chose—beer parlors, burlesque shows, gambling houses—I could not share with him and did not want our children to experience. Consequently, a great gulf arose between us that widened and deepened as the years passed. Please tell young people for me, 'The worst feature of a marriage like this is not what such a partner will do to you, bad as that may be. The worst is what he or she cannot do for you. The loneliness and emptiness in your heart and home is unbearable.'"

There was a moment of silence after she finished, and I asked, "But when you discovered you were involved in a marriage such as you have described, why did you go on for twenty years in such a union? I am sure many young people who may hear your story will ask this question."

Sadly she told me, "By the time I realized the nature of my situation, the children had begun to arrive, and from then on I never could find a time when to turn back wouldn't cause more suffering for others than for me just to go on."

This tragic experience brought home to me the reality of the chasm that can grow wide and deep between persons here in this life. In spite of the loneliness and emptiness of such a relationship, many may feel the necessity of staying together in this life because they are bound, as was Mrs. O'Neil, by ties and obligations such as marriage, that are implicit in our sexual natures and our consequent social obligations. Jesus taught, however, that we shed these material bonds with the incident of death, and on the other side will have the privilege of associating with those who attract and hold us to them only by what they are, and by the joy we experience in being together. Consider the story in Matthew 22:23f. When the Sadducees inquired concerning the woman who had married seven husbands, "In the resurrection, therefore, to which of the seven will she be wife?" Jesus answered, "You are wrong, because you know neither the scriptures nor the power of God. For in the resurrection they neither marry nor are given in marriage.'' The implication for me is clear: after death it may well be that many wives will walk away from husbands and husbands from wives, brothers from sisters and children from parents, without ever looking back. For years they have been living in different worlds, separated by great chasms which no one can cross. But they have remained together because of bonds that belong to this present world—bonds that are incident to these physical bodies and family relationships to which we have fallen heir. But in the resurrection we all will be bound alone by spiritual ties, and ''Abraham's bosom'' will be inhabited only by people who belong there and love to be there, like hummingbirds that are drawn together by the nectar in a flower garden. Those, on the other hand, who find themselves ''in Hades . . . being in torment,'' will be separated off, not because an angry God decrees it, but because they have developed such depraved tastes and interests during this life that they would be as miserable and out of place with the things of heaven as a buzzard would be among hummingbirds in a flower bed.

At this point our Spiritualist friends have come forward with a meaningful concept that speaks with point and challenge to all of us. They designate as ''earth-bound'' those spirits who, during their life here, have interested themselves only in pursuits involving the physical body. The only desires and joys they appreciate are related to eating, drinking, smoking, sex indulgence, acquiring money, or achieving status according to material standards. Whatever makes an appeal to them must do so through the same five senses possessed by their dogs. Then suddenly they experience death, lose their bodies, and pass out of this material environment. In this transition they suddenly lose everything they know about and care for, or in which they have the remotest interest. Now what are they to do? Quite literally they are ''lost,'' and according to the Spiritualist point of view, they frantically hover about the living who still are participating in bodily gratifications in an attempt to gain satisfaction vicariously through others' indulgences. This concept purports to throw light on Jesus' story: ''When the unclean spirit has gone out of a man, he passes through waterless places seeking rest, but he finds none. Then he says, 'I will return to my house from which I came''' (Matt. 12:43).

The plight of these ''earthbound'' is similar to that of a chain-smoking nicotine addict who went to the far north woods with a camping party, crossed a stormy lake, and suddenly discovered when on the other side that in the near capsize of their

45

boat he had lost his entire supply of cigarettes. Panic at once seized his mind and completely obliterated all other consid- erations. While his companions were eager and enthusiastic about going on to the fishing grounds ahead, he could only look back feverishly and desperately, pace the lakeshore, and beg for someone to return him to where his passion could be gratified. It may well be that along the path of this thought lies one facet of the "Hell" which long has troubled many sincere Christians.

This brings us to still another question regarding what it will be like on the other side. "Will there be opportunity for growth, change, and possible conversion and transformation of character after death?" This query has evoked much thought and volumes of lengthy sermons through the centuries. Our Protestant fathers on the whole rejected vehemently the idea of "a second chance," opportunity for reformation and salvation after death. They took this position because they believed such a view would cut the nerve of Christian evangelism and morality here and now and would lead sinners to remain joined to their idols, deferring their decision for Christ and the Christian life to "the sweet by-and-by." Personally, I am convinced that this is not valid reasoning, nor is it in accord either with biblical teaching or with the spirit of our Lord. In my own youth I heard clergymen quite generally assuring us that we all "grow along together until harvest" here, but at the moment of death are instantly and permanently judged to be "Children of the Devil" or "Children of Light." Accordingly we are ushered at once either into heaven and eternal bliss or to hell and endless torment.

My mind has long since rejected this image of salvation and damnation. While I was in grade school, I would listen to the impressive soloists at revival meetings sing, "I dreamed that the great judgment morning had dawned and the trumpet had blown," and would cringe at the idea of God and the relationship to his children it presented. Finally, when the chorus of that song came to a crescendo, the very thunderings of Sinai seemed to crash about us as we heard, "Then O, what a weeping and wailing when the lost were told of their fate! They cried for the rocks and the mountains; they prayed, but their prayers were too late!" The better I became acquainted with Jesus Christ, the more certain I became that this entire picture, and the motivation to Christian conduct it attempted to provide, were both ineffective and out of accord with the nature of God as revealed in the life and teachings of Jesus.

It was during my early high school days that a graphic incident occurred in our community that constituted a turning point in my thinking in this regard. A tragic event involving two young men I knew quite well banished completely from my philosophy of religion the concepts of heaven and hell as places of permanent residence to which we are assigned irrevocably at the moment of death. These two young men of our quiet and orderly neighborhood had gained the reputation of being ''wild rowdies'' and ''sensuous rounders.'' Late one night they were coming home after a fling of drunken revelry in a neighboring town, racing their Model-T Ford with the throttle wide open. Suddenly they encountered a sharp turn in the country road that they were unable to negotiate. The car was wrecked, and both boys were hurled to the roadside. Pete landed on a plot of grass, and walked away from the accident with only minor bruises. Butch, however, plunged headfirst into a bridge abutment and was instantly killed.

Etched in my memory to this very day is the horror of Butch's funeral in our village church. First there was the grim tolling of the bell nineteen times to indicate his age. Then gathered the silent crowd that filled not only the church but the yard and roadway out front. The bleak, unadorned casket came next, with pitifully few flowers, and the hushed awe of the stricken family following it blended all into the total atmosphere of morbid hopelessness. The preacher, out of what I am sure he considered to be the kindness of his heart, made no personal reference whatever to the departed. He devoted his effort completely to delivering an exhortation to repentance and Christian affiliation, obviously with the insinuation that otherwise the unheeding might have descend upon them the unspeakable doom that had overtaken Butch.

Pete, however, because of the impact the accident had on his life, like the prodigal son of Jesus' parable, ''came to himself,'' straightened up, married one of the finest girls in our community, became a deacon in the church, and won the respect of all who knew him. Then came World War I, and Pete was the first to leave our community for ''over there.'' We all saw him off with a memorable farewell that mingled tears with flag-waving and spirited war songs. But only a few months later came the shocking news to his wife and family that for our little community drained all the glamour out of ''Good-bye Broadway, Hello France.'' Pete had been killed in action on the battlefront, and his flag-draped casket was being shipped home. How can I hope adequately to describe his funeral service? Once more the church and its environs were crowded, but what a difference in atmosphere from the day we buried Butch! Flowers were banked high on the church rostrum. Conversation was fluent, and expressions of sorrow and respect mingled with a profusion of roses and lilies, all speaking eloquently of love and hope. The preacher spoke exclusively about Pete, his church life and work, his supreme sacrifice offered for his country, and his present glory in that "beautiful isle of somewhere."

By the time we reached the cemetery, I was so absorbed by the disturbing questions bombarding my mind that I failed to hear Pete's grave-side committal. Instead, I was over in a back corner of that burial ground staring at a forlorn grave where Butch's remains lay, barren even of a modest tombstone, to say nothing of a flower or fern. The question I was facing was, "Why should everyone be so certain that Butch was suffering the torments of endless hell and Pete enjoying the glories of eternal heaven? Would there be anything even approaching fairness in such an arrangement? Was it Butch's fault that while both he and Pete were living precisely the same kind of life, and then were involved in the same accident, that he should have struck a bridge abutment instead of the plot of grass that cushioned Pete's fall? Would a great and good God, the loving Father portrayed in the life and teachings of Jesus, conceivably ordain that an eternity of bliss for Pete but an eternity of torture for Butch should turn on such a purely accidental circumstance? My very soul rebelled at such a concept, and I was sure I heard my Master saying, "I am the good shepherd. A good shepherd loves his sheep, all of them, and will search for one that is lost until he finds it"*(See John 10:7f)*.

From that moment to the present, I have known in my heart that "Hell" is not doom, but discipline. I believe that when Peter told us our Lord "preached to the spirits in prison, who formerly did not obey," it was done in the possibility and expectation that those who had been cleansed by the fires they had experienced since their death, and who in consequence had become responsive to an appeal to righteousness, might have the privilege of rising up out of their miseries into the realm of joy and light. As Emmet Fox once expressed it, "Both Heaven and Hell have swing doors." I think they do indeed, and I believe that it is equally as possible to fall out of heaven as it is and always will be to climb out of hell.

I believe the Roman Catholic Christians were groping after an answer precisely to the dilemma I faced in that old country churchyard when they developed the concept of purgatory. They recognized that virtually none are so totally bad when they die that they merit no consideration whatever, deserving only to be tortured in hell forever for their sins. On the other hand, they realized that just as few, if indeed any at all, are so pure and spotless in character that they could be introduced directly into a perfect heaven without contaminating it on the one hand and searing their souls on the other. Therefore, as an attempted solution for this predicament, they inserted an intermediate state, where those too good for hell could take advantage of preparatory disciplines and seize upon the opportunity to cleanse their spirits and thereby escape eternal damnation; and where those not good enough for a heavenly state could take advantage of this forbearance of our Lord, seizing the opportunity for the spiritual growth to make it into heaven.

As I mentioned previously, our Protestant forebears violently resisted this doctrine because they felt it would lead sinners to procrastinate and defer their acceptance of Christ's salvation, insisting they would enjoy the pleasures of sin throughout their earthly lives here, and then repent and make it into glory anyway in the hereafter. They also rejected the Catholic form of the doctrine because they felt that purgatory, with its concept of loved ones there suffering tortures from which they might be released through prayers and rituals provided by the church and its priests, lent itself to distortion and even to racketeering on the part of a less than holy priesthood. They were perhaps justly fearful that the unscrupulous might exact heavy tribute from bereaved families and friends in promise of receiving forgiveness and release for "the souls in prison." Unquestionably, at low levels of ecclesiastical practice, such advantage has often been taken of this doctrine. This regrettable fact, however, in no way influences the fundamental truth inherent in the purgatory concept.

To indicate the degree to which some Protestant ministers and leaders sometimes become perplexed over how to handle their sharply defined, black-and-white separation of all people into the "saved" on the one hand and the "damned" on the other at the instance of death, I recall the depth of my own minister-father's concern on the occasion of the death of Teddy Roosevelt. It was the virility and dynamism of this national hero that so attracted my father, and when he heard of Teddy's death, he sat down under his favorite shade tree in our yard and was respectfully silent for a long time. Then, staring thoughtfully into space, he reflected audibly, "Now what will the Lord ever do with Teddy? He's too good for hell; but if they try to consign him to those gold streets of heaven and hand him a robe and harp, he'll blow up the place before we even get his funeral over."

I thank God for the clarity of my conviction that eternal life, on this side of death or on the other side, involves constant and never-ending growth, change, and development. When we again see our Jeanne for example, the daughter who left us as an eager and starry-eyed youngster at the age of fourteen, do I expect her to be just as she was thirty years ago? At first thought we might insist upon having her so, but mature reflection quickly reveals that such a desire would be prompted only by our own selfish desires and nostalgic preferences. The instant we recognize that our love for her must constitute sensitivity to and concern for *her* feelings and welfare, for *her* sake and not for ours, then we will prefer instantly that in the intervening years she will have grown and developed at least as much on that side of death as we have changed on this side.

This Christian concept, in terms of the spirit of Jesus Christ and his portrayal of the nature of God, gives me hope to impart to the families of individuals who died while living useless or shameful lives, as well as to those who died the death of the righteous. Otherwise, what could I as a minister of Jesus Christ say to the brokenhearted father and mother of the young man whose mutilated body recently lay in a casket where I had been summoned to preside at the funeral? While attempting to burglarize a store in our city, this youthful delinquent had been surprised by the police. When commanded to halt, he threw a vicious piece of steel at an officer and then started running away bent over low in the darkness. The officer fired one bullet, aimed over the fugitive's head to impress his command, and again shouted "Halt!" Just as the gun fired, however, the young man straightened up, and the bullet passed directly through his head. This disgraceful and highly publicized event was for that boy only the terminal incident in an inglorious life of rebellion, truancy, and crime. As the grieving and quite respectable family, of which he was the one black sheep in the fold, looked up eagerly for a ray of hope in their hour of sorrow, how grateful I was to be able to tell them of a Good Shepherd who has announced that he will search for his sheep *until he finds it*. I assured them further that by the time they see this erring young man again, it is quite possible he will have learned lessons in the second grade he failed to grasp in the first, and by then possibly exceed any of them in virtuous and commendable character.

By no means, as I view it, does this point of view cut the nerve of either morality or evangelism, nor will it lead anyone to defer acceptance of the Christian life. Rather, when we realize that heaven is a state of union and intimacy with God and his other children, we will understand that the sooner we get into that blessed relationship the sooner we will find real joy and happiness. Conversely, the sooner we repent and turn our backs on thoughts, words, and actions that injure others and separate us from them, from God, and from ourselves, the quicker we will find release from the hell of separation and loneliness that is already making life unbearable for us.

Dr. G. Campbell Morgan once told of a young man in his study who said sadly, "I've come to take my stand for Christ. I've firmly decided to become a Christian, but it sure is going to go against the grain!" In quick response Dr. Morgan answered,

> You're dead wrong, sir! In the worldly life you have described to me as your experience to date, you already have been going against the grain of our Father's world. Your situation has been analogous to a marble rolling crosswise on a corrugated tin roof. Now you are planning to change your direction and go with the grain, and you soon will learn what Jesus meant when he said, "Come to me, all who labor and are heavy-laden, and I will give you rest." He was not indicating that you should lie down. He meant that now you will find relief from the wear and tear that comes to all who are living at cross-currents with the universe and have been going against the grain.

This point of view furnished every incentive an intelligent and responsible person should require to induce him to take the high road in life instead of the low, and to begin that way of life at the earliest possible moment. When we realize that our joy and happiness, both in this life and the next, are dependent upon our getting "in tune with the infinite," establishing respectful and loving relationships with God and other persons, and of "going with the grain" of life, we will know that we should begin this way of living with the Lord at once, realizing that the longer we put it off the greater is our loss. We furthermore will discover that the appeal to all of a loving Father standing in the lane yearning for the return of his prodigal son, and of a Good Shepherd resolved to search for his rebellious sheep "until he finds it," will furnish more effective motivation for repentance and Christian character than fear of eternal punishment has ever provided.

# Chapter 5

## Bad and Good Grief

The message I want to share with you in this chapter I know to be of keen interest to everyone. I have indeed learned that when I want to reach the largest possible audience, I speak to broken hearts. Lord Tennyson wrote a wealth of poetry, all of high quality and unquestioned excellence; but by far his most widely known and best loved lines tell us, "For though from out our bourne of Time and Place the flood may bear me far, I hope to see my Pilot face to face when I have crossed the bar."[8] And again, "The stately ships go on to their haven under the hill, but O for the touch of a vanished hand, and the sound of a voice that is still!"[9] Notice that both of these deal directly with the universal experiences of death and grief.

I walked recently through the very old Walnut Grove Cemetery near our city where most of the bodies were returned to the dust from which they came more than a hundred years ago. I was impressed with the large number of children and young people buried there. Many teenagers were among them, and even a larger number of young husbands or wives in their twenties or thirties. I paused to picture the scene of heartbreak and sorrow that once had been enacted at each of these gravesides, for unquestionably the pain is more acute when older family members are compelled to say good-bye to the younger ones. Then suddenly I found myself standing before a stone that bore the striking epitaph, "These all died in faith, not having received the promises." I sat down on a neighboring slab where I could stare at these lines meditatively. I recalled that these had indeed died not having received hospital treatment, smallpox vaccination, pure water and food protection, blood transfusions, or oxygen inhalation in their hours of critical need. But I recalled just as vividly that those broken-hearted fathers, mothers, brothers, and sisters dried their tears, squared their shoulders, and went back to their farms, schools, and factories to hew out for us of this generation a wealth of privileges that to them were only promises seen from afar. I realized also

53

that, except for their courage and wisdom in facing sorrow and grief, they would have been demoralized by their losses and we deprived of our blessings.

Now let me ask pointedly: Do we of this generation do as well with the healing of our memories as they did with theirs? Do we today adjust as well as our pioneer fathers and mothers did to the losses in companionship we still must suffer through the tragic death experiences that certainly will come to most of our firesides sooner or later? I am fearful that the richness of our life in this affluent land has made some of us soft, and that we tend much more readily to fold up in the face of trial. Accordingly, it seems proper to set forth here some of the wholesome feelings and attitudes in a time of grief that may be expected to lead us through this "valley of the shadow of death," and bring us out on the other side into awareness and enjoyment of the sunshine once more.

It also is entirely right that we speak about grief, for this certainly is one experience that must be shared if it is to accomplish its purpose and then retire from dominating our lives. Anyone who insists upon remaining alone in his grief will accomplish just that. He will remain alone, and will also remain in his grief. I further feel that I have some measure of right to speak on this subject, because a minister is probably more "acquainted with grief" than any other person. This is particularly true of the specialized ministry of the clinically trained hospital chaplain, but is little less so in the case of the faithful parish pastor who keeps close to the lives of his people. The doctor and funeral director are in contact with stricken families to be sure, but their services generally end abruptly when the patient dies and is buried, while the minister only begins his best service to the bereaved at this point.

First of all, let me define "grief," so that we may know clearly what it is we are speaking about. Grief is not evil that good people of faith should shun, nor is it an evidence of emotional weakness or instability of which the strong and responsible should be ashamed. In the infinite wisdom and providence of God, grief has been given to men and women as a necessary and highly valuable process with a definite purpose to fulfill, and one which almost every person alive will need on one or more occasions during a lifetime. *Grief is the physical, intellectual, and spiritual process by means of which an individual is gradually released from the bonds that lashed him or her so inseparably to some other person or circumstance that life seems empty and meaningless when the beloved has been removed by death.*

Our Christian faith teaches clearly that the best treatment for this problem is prevention. The first commandment lays down the directive, "You shall have no other gods before me," and it is only when we first ignore or break this law of life that we allow ourselves to become vulnerably dependent upon anybody or anything so fleeting or fragile as another human individual. Jesus told us it is a foolish person who builds his house on a sandbar that can be washed out at any moment. Dr. M. H. Lichliter, a onetime ministerial colleague, once delivered a sermon on the theme, "Sit Loose to the Changing Order of Things." Indeed, we all need to walk through our lives frequently checking the price tags, and if we find "other gods" at or near the head of the list, give our scale of life priorities and values prayerful rearrangement. My wife and I have long since formed the habit of walking through our lives from time to time to practice giving up anything that is becoming indispensable or critically important to us. We understand that we do not actually have to give up these people, things, or circumstances to which we have become attached, but we do have to be *willing* to do so. This spiritual discipline has helped us learn what it means to be "leaning on the everlasting arms" and building our life security on God, the one firm and dependable rock that alone can provide safe and secure foundation for anyone's happiness and usefulness.

But prepare ourselves as we may, we do all love; and just as inevitably we do all lose on occasion. Our hearts get broken and bleed, and we desperately need assistance for our recovery if our lives are not to sink into depression or despair or "come unglued," as some would say. Prevention of this tragedy is precisely what the grief process is designed by a considerate God to achieve for us. We must face the fact, however, that there is bad as well as good grief. Bad grief is usually good grief that has become arrested in its normal process—grief that perpetuates one phase of bereavement long past the period of its usefulness and makes a permanent stumbling block of what was intended to be a temporary stepping stone.

Let me offer two pointed examples of bad grief. Dr. Gerald Heard, one of the great minds and spirits of our generation, suffered the loss of his mother when he was born. His grief-stricken father, in response to this tragedy, closed up his beloved wife's room, draped her picture with a black veil, resented the baby that had occasioned the catastrophe, and forbade that even the name of his lost loved one should ever be mentioned in the household. As a result of this crystallization of a grief reaction, that house ceased to be a home and became for years a chilling morgue of cold, silent sorrow. There probably is hardly one of us who has not known some person or family who has sunk into the mire of bad grief in similar fashion, to the ruination of a happy home and damage to all the personalities involved.

Again, as our own grieving family returned home from the funeral parlor the night after our daughter Jeanne died, an older minister knocked at our door. He had driven many miles across our state to set a basket of flowers on our living room floor and share an important message with us.

"I just had to come," he told us, "because I know how you feel. We lost our little girl seven years ago. Just this week my wife said to me, 'It is worse for me now than it was the day after she went away.' For her, I am sure this is true. I also believe I know why it is true, and this is why I had to come for this visit with you. When we returned home after the funeral service for our little girl, I wanted to give away all her clothes, toys, books, and other belongings. We were surrounded by very poor families, almost all of whom had children who needed these things desperately and could have used them gratefully. But not my wife! She refused to part with a single article, gathered our little girl's things together, and put them all in a big bureau drawer. From that hour to this there has hardly been a day or night when she has not gone to that bureau, pulled out the drawer, picked up those little articles one by one, and cried over them. As a consequence she has kept the wound in her heart so wide open that after seven years she can say, 'It is worse for me today than it was the day after she left us.'"

This is a typical instance of "bad grief," and in a similarly arrested grief situation lives a mother in our city whose husband died suddenly four years ago. She went home from the funeral service to pull down the blinds and think of nothing but the cemetery where the body of her beloved is buried. At first she went to visit his grave once, then twice, and now three or four times a week. Her children feel rejected, believing she has no love for them because of her complete absorption in thoughts of their late father. Then a few weeks ago she began getting up in the middle of the night, often only partially clothed, to start walking to the cemetery. At present she is committed to our state mental hospital and is under psychiatric treatment. Her situation, while more extreme than many, sets forth clearly what I mean when I indicate that we face the possibility of bad as well as good grief.

But, thank God, in many other lives grief is accomplishing its work effectively all about us every day. Quite generally it follows the pattern I shall now describe, although by no means do all individuals pass through the grief stages in this order. Indeed, many persons will shuttle back and forth from one step to another in the process, may skip one or more of them completely, or will seem to be in several of these moods simultaneously. Most individuals, however, will at one time or another experience these phases of the grief experience, and it is helpful to understand them in order better to facilitate the process in our own lives, or to assist its progress in others. I am most grateful for permission from Granger E. Westberg to use his outline of the grief experience as a basis for my own analysis. His book is entitled, *Good Grief—A Constructive Approach to the Problem of Loss,* published by Fortress Press.

First comes SHOCK. Thank God for this blessed, natural anesthetic he has provided for his children, to help carry us through the initial, critical impact on our minds and spirits that accompanies tragedy or loss. There will be hours, or even days and weeks, when you will find yourself saying, "It doesn't seem real . . . it just can't be true!" This means that to a degree and for a time, we are out of touch with reality. Psychiatrists designate this "the denial mechanism," which the human mind puts into action to cushion itself against pain or loss that otherwise would be intolerable. During World War II a fine young man, an only child of an attractive, suburban couple of our city that had centered their whole lives on him, plunged into the ocean in a "Hell-Diver" plane he was piloting and was killed in action in the southwest Pacific. His mother refused to believe the report of his death, and even became angry at friends who attempted to express sympathy. For months she watched the mail and listened continually for communication from him that would assure her he was alive and coming home. Her "bad grief" held her in the shock and denial stage for more than a year until she finally collapsed physically. Only then did she become able to move on through subsequent stages of the normal grief process and toward recovery.

Next comes EMOTIONAL RELEASE. This is the time when the tears flow, and cries or sobs break forth in profusion. It is quite important that no friend or counselor try to dam up this flow of emotional release by protesting, "There, there now! Don't cry! Be brave!" How much more helpful it is to shed a sincerely sympathetic tear along with the bereaved, extend an affectionate arm or shoulder, and encourage him or her to express the grief feelings freely. An old McGuffey Reader our grandfathers studied in one-room schools told a story of a proud oak tree that refused to bend its head before any storm. When the peak and fury of a violent tempest broke over it one day, however, it came crashing down, never to rise again. Nearby stood in contrast a slender, humble aspen. When the winds came roaring through its branches, it bowed itself lower and lower, until at the height of the blast it was almost on the ground. But when the wind and the rain finally subsided and the sun beamed forth once more, it rose straight up to its original stance, completely uninjured by the experience. Indeed, it was even a little stronger than before by reason of the trial it had undergone. This is a meaningful parable for human minds subjected to the onslaughts of tragedy and sorrow. We are told in John 11:35 that "Jesus wept." Many are acquainted with this verse of scripture, but few know that the occasion of his exhibition of emotional release was at the graveside of Lazarus, his good friend who had just died. Paul is often quoted as telling us, "Sorrow not!" But in fact, this is not what he advised at all. Rather he wrote, "Sorrow not as those who have no hope," and this is an entirely different matter. It is highly important that we know that an outpouring of expressions of sorrow at a time of loss through death is a normal and altogether desirable part of the effective grief process.

Now we are likely to encounter NEGATIVE CONCENTRA-TION. The bereaved at this point wants to talk, hear, and think of nothing but the lost object of affection. While the grieving one is in this stage, it is unwise to attempt to divert him or her from preoccupation with the loss by telling funny stories or airily chatting about the latest news headline or weather report. Just now this person needs to talk about the beloved, and very seriously requires some concerned and valued friend who will share the conversation and be a good listener. An old Jewish custom provided for "the first meal of consolation" following each funeral ceremony. When the family returned from the cemetery, neighbors would have food prepared. The rabbi, a number of family members, and close friends would be gathered, and by prescribed rule the conversation had to be exclusively about the deceased. This was a very wise provision and a custom that might be profitably adopted and emulated on a wide scale today.

Next come the PHYSICAL SYMPTOMS. By now the continued inner tensions of spirit have taken their toll on the body, and there is noticeable impairment of digestion, circulation, heart action, and breathing. The griefstricken one does not want to eat or drink, sleeps fitfully if at all, usually complains of "a weight in my chest," and heaves frequent sighs to relax tensions and assist respiration. If through "bad grief" one or more of the acute stages of the grieving process is prolonged these functional discomforts may turn to real pains occasioned by congestion and organic illness.

By this time the bereaved is likely to sink into acute DEPRESSION AND WITHDRAWAL. The whole world seems to fall in, the future appears completely black, and the day is dark and dreary. When the fabric of one's life has had interwoven into its cherished pattern a dominant thread, and suddenly that cord is torn out and removed, it is natural that the remaining strands will fail to present a design that seems meaningful or even tolerable. The bereaved may even withdraw from life as far as it is possible to do so. The thought is often entertained that it would be disloyal to the departed if the surviving one should go places, do things, or give indication of enjoying anything.

A few years ago a fine elder in our church congregation lost his beautiful young wife whom he adored. Her illness had lasted only a few days. On the morning following the funeral he walked and walked, finally coming to himself in the heart of our city. Suddenly, as he reported to me, "I realized, *The street cars are running! Why should the street cars be running?*" Then he heard some men actually laughing and joking as they came out of a hotel lobby, and his impulse was to rush up and choke them. *"Why should street cars be running and anyone be laughing, when the world has come to a standstill and life is over?"* was his overwhelming thought. He then began to make the cemetery his retreat, and spent more than a year in withdrawal from life. He would look at the familiar scenes around him and see all of them as strange and disassociated from him. He told me one day, "See that tree? It and I used to be in the same world!" He had been a singer and socially the life of the party on every occasion, but now he was immersed in a lonely flood of depression, entombed in a cold, dark cell of withdrawal and separation. This condition is quite normal, and not to be a matter of concern unless it is unduly protracted.

Now we witness the center of the stage being usurped by GUILT. The grieving person seems completely obsessed with mistakes he or she made when the loved one was present. Repeatedly friends will hear such outbursts as, "If only I had refused to permit that operation!" or perhaps, "If I just hadn't scolded Mother so!" The primary problem in dealing with these guilt feelings arises out of the fact of ambivalence, mixed feelings toward the deceased which most grieving persons definitely have but refuse to admit. In almost every instance, we can be certain the loved and lost individual had good and bad characteristics, and that there was a part of the bereaved that loved and a part that always resented or even hated the deceased. We also must recognize that the incident of death does not suddenly transform earthy people into shining saints, gloriously transfigured. Mother may indeed have been selfish and demanding to an unreasonable degree, quite cranky during her illness as well as long before it, and may have very well deserved the reprimands and disciplinings she received. Until the grief-stricken can recognize the truth of this fact, guilt feelings cannot properly be resolved.

Of course there is often very real guilt to deal with, not just guilt feelings, and this fact may seriously complicate the matter and impede the normal progress of the grief process. Too often the situation prevails where the one remaining knows full well that he or she mistreated the departed in ways that haunt and disturb, and committed unpardoned sins the memory of which now march by at night in scarlet procession. For such a tormented soul there is always available the forgiveness of God for past sins or mistakes, and opportunity through a penitent attitude in God's presence to talk to and restore a wholesome fellowship in spirit with the one who was wronged.

Next we will probably encounter HOSTILITY. At this state in the grief process the mind of the bereaved seeks an outlet in rage and anger, perhaps toward the doctor who "never should have performed that operation in the first place," toward the nurse or hospital who "neglected Mother terribly," or even the minister who "should have given her a lot more attention during her illness." It is rare that a sorrowing person will realize that his real resentment is against God and life in general that has dealt this cruel blow, and that he or she unconsciously is only working out resentful feelings against these who are most handy. Eventually the necessity for this emotional catharsis will pass, and the hostile attitudes will disappear. In the meantime, a certain amount of such vehemence should be expected; and when it occurs it should be generously tolerated as being at least mildly therapeutic, and not permitted to sever friendships for the years ahead.

By now we should begin to observe GRADUAL REALIZA-TION. At this juncture, brief snatches of objectivity begin to break through into the consciousness of the one borne down with grief. He or she may be heard saying, "I have been acting foolishly, haven't I?" Quite often the dark moods of negative concentration, depression, guilt, and withdrawal will seem to break up momentarily like a rift in the clouds on an overcast day, allowing the sunbeams of life and love to break through. The man I mentioned earlier, who practically lived for three months in the cemetery where his beautiful, young wife was buried, experienced this critical moment in his recovery:

One day he was planting a flower on her grave and choking on the lump in his throat as usual. Suddenly he heard her voice speaking so clearly and in such familiar tone that he turned around quickly, fully expecting to see her standing behind him. She had said, "Honey! What *are* you doing out *here?*" That was all, but it was enough. It marked the glorious moment when the sun of reality broke through the clouds of his grief to convince him that life still held something worthwhile for him. He testifies that he straightened up, looked at the trees, the fence, even the grass around him, and suddenly they were in the same world with him again. Everything was changed, and a feeling of foolishness and embarrassment for being there swept over him. He went directly to his car, drove home, and never visited that cemetery again except once a year on Memorial Day. When he reached his empty house that had been their happy home, loneliness and longing still deluged his spirit; but the spell was broken. Gradually the positive and realistic attitudes grew in both clarity and frequency, and he was on his way to recovery.

Finally, thank God, if all goes well we see the grieving one experience READJUSTMENT TO REALITY. There will always be a scar, of course, and life will never be quite the same as before. By now, however, life can go on—more understanding of others in trouble, more sympathetic, and possibly more beautiful than ever.

I remember walking with my father in a very old cemetery during my high school days. Together we were reading the interesting epitaphs on the weather-beaten stones, many of which were more than a hundred years old. Suddenly we found ourselves scanning the dim lettering that memorialized a man who had died before the Civil War. Beside his resting place was the grave of his young wife of twenty-four years, and on her stone this grief-stricken husband had carved the plaintive line, "The light of my life has gone out!" As I read the sentiment and pondered the situation sadly, my father, who was a few feet farther ahead looking at the gravestone of a second wife, remarked with a twinkle in his eye, "Don't feel too badly son; I see he found another match!" Thank God for the effective work of the grief process that enabled the light to come back on in that man's life, and in the lives of innumerable other persons who temporarily have been plunged into darkness by loss through death of one they loved.

The classical biblical example of this successful readjustment to

61

reality undoubtedly is set forth in the life of David *(2 Sam. 12:15f)*. This great old king was so stricken with grief when his baby fell critically ill that he wept, fasted, prayed, and lay day after day on the ground, oblivious to all around him. When the child eventually died, the servants were afraid to tell him. They said to one another, ''Behold, while the child was yet alive, we spoke to him, and he did not listen to us; how then can we say to him the child is dead? He may do himself some harm.''

But noticing their whisperings and being sensitive to the change in mood in the household, David asked, ''Is the child dead?'' They answered him, ''Yes, he is dead.'' With this David arose, bathed himself, dressed, and went into the house of the Lord for worship. Then he returned to his own house and called for food. When he had finished eating, he launched into his accumulated work.

In the face of such inexplicable conduct the perplexed servants asked in amazement, ''What is this thing that you have done? You fasted and wept for the child while it was alive; but when the child died, you arose and ate food.'' Then came David's priceless answer that mercifully has winged its way down to us through 3,000 intervening years. He told his astonished servants, ''While the child was still alive, I fasted and wept, for I said, 'Who knows whether the Lord will be gracious to me, that the child may live?' But now he is dead; why should I fast? Can I bring him back again? I shall go to him, but he will not return to me.''

# NOTES

1. Henry Wadsworth Longfellow, "A Psalm of Life."
2. Francis Quarles, "Epigram."
3. Henry Wadsworth Longfellow, "The Village Blacksmith."
4. Lyman Abbott, *Reminiscences*. Boston: Houghton Mifflin Company, 1915. p. 493.
5. Harry Emerson Fosdick, *Rufus Jones Speaks to Our Time*. New York: MacMillan, Inc., 1951. p. 277.
6. Harry Emerson Fosdick, *Adventurous Religion*. Blue Ribbon Books, 1926. p. 18.
7. L. Harold DeWolf, *A Theology of the Living Church*. New York: Harper and Row, 1960. p. 219.
8. Alfred, Lord Tennyson, "Crossing the Bar."
9. Alfred, Lord Tennyson, "Break, Break, Break."